THE
LEADERSHIP
PLAYBOOK

Become Your Team's
Most Valuable Leader

JAMY BECHLER

ISBN: 0-9992125-0-8
ISBN-13: 978-0-9992125-0-9

MOSCOW ☙ HEIGHTS
📖 PUBLISHING 📖

Cover photo: Courtesy of Indiana Wesleyan University and athletic director
Mark DeMichael. The photo is of the IWU men's basketball locker room.
To find out more about Indiana Wesleyan University athletics, go to
www.IWUwildcats.com

Online Resources: To access the free online resources that come with your
purchase of the book, please visit www.TheLeadershipPlaybook.com and
use the code "Online".

CONTENTS

ACKNOWLEDGMENTS

You can't write a book by yourself. Just like a team is needed to play sports, a team was needed for to put this book together. I want to thank some of the people that helped out with The Leadership Playbook. Your help was truly appreciated. I could not have crossed "publish a book" off of my bucket list without you. If I inadvertently left your name off this list, please accept my apologies – it is like the acceptance speeches at the Oscars, as I am sure to forget someone.

Tabitha, you were very supportive throughout the whole process and kept encouraging me to fulfill this dream. I love you!

My parents and in-laws for supporting me throughout the process and watching Jaylen at key points in the book writing process.

My brother Corey for constantly bugging me about whether or not the book was done and what was taking me so long.

My book advisory team who helped with editing and providing feedback on various ideas that I had. Thank you Andy Carter, Rashaun Warren, Jeff Turner, David Carrel, John Motherwell, Jeff Raver, Marcus Hall, Chad Hall, Denny Lehnus, Melanie Williams, Tina Smith, Jenna Everhart, and Steve Barrows.

All of my friends and family members that spread the word about the book on social media were a big help in promoting it. Thank you for using your influence.

I am honored by all of the great people that provided endorsements and testimonials about me or the book. You can see their names on the back cover or at TheLeadershipPlaybook.com

Mathoni Villegas, you did an awesome job on the book cover. It is sharp and you were very easy to work with.

The Super Coach Micheal Burt for walking me through writing my first book with his "Making of a Coach" program.

Larry Jose, my high school band teacher for kicking me out of class but not before telling me something that I'd forever remember (see chapter 3) and would lead off many of speeches that I give to student-athletes.

All of my coaches that put up with me through the years and help shape me (especially Bill Dunn, my high school varsity basketball coach, who died of cancer too young at age 47).

Judith Shannon and Judy Hale, my high school English teachers.

Cathy Hartley, my high school typing teacher. It might not have been an "academic" course but it was one of the most important classes I ever took.

Linda Rea and MaryAnn Brocket who helped me understand the art of communicating as a college student back at Hiram College.

John C. Maxwell for his integrity and desire to add value to people all across the world. As a certified John Maxwell Team Member, I am honored to be a part of something bigger than myself.

FOREWORD

When I played for Coach Bechler he valued leadership very strongly. We did a lot of drills to improve our leadership skills and also had daily quotes. Each week he would post a quote and each person had to memorize that quote and if not there was always a consequence. Leadership is very important at every level and it should be taught daily. The teams that have good leadership skills and everyone is held accountable for their actions; those teams are more likely to succeed.

One may think to play on a professional level we may not need to use our leadership skills as much because we are already pros. However, that's not the case, because we still have to use our leadership skills we were taught because it's our job. As Americans, we have to put our team in a successful position or we could be sent home, but this is when you bring everyone on board and show them how to lead as one unit.

This year (2017) I played in Sweden and my team had never had Americans and never played in the playoffs, but we knew we had to lead this team and bring everyone on board. We were two professionals on the team so our goal was to make sure everyone was unified. We made history at EOS just by leading and holding each other accountable. Leadership will bring success on and off the court so lead wherever you may go because it can be quite contagious!

VEE YOUNG
Professional Basketball Player
Martin Methodist College All-American

FOREWORD

When I was in high school I was kind of a big deal because I was a basketball player in a small town that loved its' basketball. I played varsity as an 8th grader, was Homecoming Queen my senior year, and top-10 academically in my class. Basketball was my first priority, nothing else mattered. I didn't care about the crowns or academic achievements, I ditched homecoming pictures so I could get dressed for my basketball game.

Every game was like life or death to me. I was a very aggressive player, had an attitude, and hated to lose. But I soon learned that being a leader on the court gave me the power to be a leader off it, as well. With the teaching of a wonderful, Godly woman as a mom, I knew I could use my ability for good off-the-court. It would just take me being kind to others.

It is amazing how playing sports causes so many people to follow your lead. Sure, I could score a lot of points or shut my opponent down. That came easily to me. But believe it or not, kindness was a tougher task. Sadly, that can turn you into an outcast quicker than missing a game-winning shot. I lost some friends over just speaking to people who were not part of our group of "friends" in the hallway and that was okay with me.

When I graduated from high school, my teammates gave me a book of memories. In it was an English essay that had been written about me for a class. The assignment was to write an essay on someone that was your hero. In it, the student had written about me playing basketball. However, towards the end she wrote, "but most of all she was nice". Me, a hero? Hardly - but I have kept that paper all these years as a reminder that I can make a difference and it is as simple as just being nice. You never know who is watching. Abilities are God-given but leadership is earned, make the effort because you (and others) matter.

ASHLEY (WHITTAKER) DODD
Played for Coach Bechler at Tennessee Temple University
Played for Coach Bechler in Hawaii on a college select-team.

1.
INTRODUCTION

"A year from now, you'll wish you started today."
– Karen Lamb

"There is a choice you have to make in everything you do. So keep in mind that in the end, the choice you make makes you."
– John Wooden

"You cannot change your destination overnight, but you can your direction overnight."
– Jim Rohn

This book is written with the student-athlete in mind. It is designed to help student-athletes understand how they can help their team achieve more success regardless of their role on the team. Whether a player is a freshman or senior, reserve or starter, the examples and insights in the following chapters will help walk them through the situations that they will encounter as a member of a team. Student-athletes can read the book straight through or pick out specific chapters that they are most curious about.

Even though the book is for student-athletes, coaches can gain a great deal by reading it, as well. In fact, a team's results are optimized if a coach is reinforcing and revisiting the themes and insights contained in this book throughout the season. Coaches, feel free to put the quotes that start each chapter on your bulletin board in the locker room. I love quotes and intentionally included more than normal at the start of each chapter.

Leadership training is not a one-time event. It is a continually process that a coaching staff should make an intentional part of the regular schedule. Leadership is a skill that student-athletes should be learning and practicing daily just as if they are taking batting practice or shooting free throws.

The topic of leadership oftentimes becomes cliché' and boring because we treat it either as something that most people can't obtain or don't need to obtain. Sportscasters and coaches say all the time that this team had great leadership or that team struggled with leadership but they rarely expand upon those opinions. In fact, those statements are oftentimes rooted in results-oriented thinking. We are to believe that good teams have good leadership and bad teams have poor leadership. This is neither true nor false. Sometimes talented teams win despite their tangibles and strong character teams lose because of their lack of talent.

Our goal for developing leadership is to maximize an individual and a team's potential. Talented teams might win but they don't always maximize their potential. The talented student-athletes on winning teams also don't always develop their student-athletes to be successful in life, which is a far bigger and more crucial game. A talented team can be defeated. A talented team with strong character and positive leadership is nearly unbeatable. More importantly, those individual members will have a greater likelihood to be successful in whatever they set their mind to because they have built a strong foundation and have developed positive daily habits.

If you have an average team, we want to help make you good. If you already have a good team, we want to help you become great. If you have a championship-level team, then we want you to develop even more consistency. Always improving. Continually striving for perfection, even though it is not attainable, should lead to a level of excellence that is seen in teams such as the New England Patriots, Golden State Warriors, or the University of Connecticut women's basketball team.

PERSPECTIVE

To become the leader that you were meant to be, you must look at things from a different point of view. Two stories come to my mind when thinking about perspective. The first is a little boy that is playing baseball by himself,

> "I'm the greatest baseball player in the world," a little boy boasted as he strutted around his backyard. Shouldering his

bat, he tossed a baseball up, swung, and missed. "I am the greatest ball player ever," he reiterated. He picked up the ball again, swung, and missed again. Stopping a moment to examine his bat, he stooped and picked up his ball. "I am the greatest baseball player who ever lived!" The momentum of his swing nearly knocked him down. But the ball plopped, unscathed, at his feet. "Wow!" he exclaimed. "What a pitcher!"

Mark McCormack, author of *What They Don't Teach You at Harvard Business School,* wrote a story detailing the issue of varying points of view for Entrepreneur magazine,

> "A few years ago I was standing in an airport ticket line. In front of me were two children fighting over an ice cream cone. In front of them was a woman in a mink coat. I could see this was an accident waiting to happen. Should I interfere? I was still pondering this when I heard the girl tell the boy, 'If you don't stop, Charlie, you'll get hairs from that lady's coat on your cone.'"

For most of us, the traditional way of looking at leadership is not the most effective way. Relying solely on the coach, captain(s), senior(s) or star player to be the leader will potentially leave you with an overall leadership void on your team. Positional leadership can only take a team so far. Yes, there is a need for positional leadership, but there is just as much a need for non-traditional leaders on a team. Think about any team that you have been a member of. Chances are that not every member of the team liked or respected the traditional, positional leader. If that was the case, then who was it that was leading those team members?

A team that is fully maximizing their potential has as many team members as possible that are all going in the same direction. Ideally, a team wants every member to be rowing the boat in the same direction. This is hard to accomplish if the only leaders on a team are positional leaders because they do not always earn that position with unanimous approval.

Therefore, what you will be reading in this book and getting with the free online resources are proven strategies and insights on leadership that might be different than you are used to. That is okay. If you truly want to maximize your success, then you need to be willing to do things better. Part of being better and improving is honest self-evaluation and part of self-evaluation is looking at things from a different point of view.

For example, your coach will typically give you a scouting report on the opponent prior to the next game. This is so that you can see things from a different perspective and understand your opponent. The same is true for the concepts in this book. If you want to be prepared for your next season, then you must look at things differently in order to solidify your strengths and find your weaknesses. Leadership is no different. "The way it has always been done" is what is normally said by teams and individuals that refuse to reach their potential. Their thoughts seal their fate long before their actions do.

If you want to be more successful and ultimately help your team have more success, then you need to see yourself as a leader. Your team will probably have captains but that doesn't mean that you can't be the captain of you. If you are leading yourself – which really is just doing what you are supposed to do, then you will give yourself a chance to be successful. When you are successful at leading yourself, then you make it more possible to influence your teammates.

This is when you become your team's Most Valuable Leader. When your team has lots of players doing what is necessary to be the MVL, then the sky is the limit for your team's success.

2.
FOUNDATIONAL
PRINCIPLES

"Champions don't beat themselves. If you want to win, do the ordinary things better than anyone else does – day in and day out. We're not going to fool people or out-scheme them. We're just going to outplay them. Because we'll know what we're doing. When we get into a critical situation, we won't have to think. We'll play fast and fundamentally sound."
– Chuck Noll

"Ninety-nine percent of leadership failures are failures of character."
– General Norman Schwarzkopf

"To win it all, a team has to be obsessive about the fundamentals and the little things."
– Joe Gibbs

"We are what we repeatedly do. Excellence then is not an act but a habit."
– Aristotle

"I have no choice about whether or not I have Parkinson's Disease; I have nothing but a choice about how I react to it."
– Michael J. Fox

Every well-built house starts with a solid foundation. Every player should start off learning the fundamentals of their sport. It is the same way with leadership. Leadership is influence. In order to have a positive influence on yourself and others, you must have a foundation. You need some core principles and values that you live by and internalize. This foundation must become part of you or else you will fall short of reaching your potential as a player and as a leader.

SUCCESS IS A CHOICE

Most choices that we have in life are simple. Knowing the right thing to do is not the hard part, choosing to do the right thing is the difficult part. I love Diet Dr. Pepper, Kit Kats, and Twizzlers. These are my favorite snacks. However, a bottle of water, granola bar, and apple are better for me and will help me have more lasting energy. Most choices we have in life are not real tricky. Good sleep, not good sleep, hydration, watching film, not drinking, not smoking or working out – we know whether these are good choices or not.

Success is a choice. Do you want to be successful? Success is a choice. Unfortunately, so is failure. Every choice that we make in life either complicates or simplifies our life – usually in the area of fulfilling our goals and aspirations. Sometimes you've got to do some things you don't want to do so that you can accomplish things that you want to accomplish.

Remember, knowing the right thing to do is not the hard part, choosing to do the right thing is the difficult part. The choices you make today affect you tomorrow, next month, next year. Your results during the season will be a direct result of what you did during those months leading up to the season. Your results in a game will have more to do with the practices in the previous week than the actual game.

Your daily choices lead to daily habits which lead to success or failure. Who you want to be in the future and what you want to accomplish is determined by what you do today, tomorrow, next month, next year. This is the same with us when it comes to our daily choices shaping our habits. Eventually, we will have either winning habits or losing habits. It is up to you. Your choice.

INTEGRITY

Integrity is the building block and most basic tenet to all other traits. If you are not an ethical person with a solid foundation of doing the right thing consistently, then you will not be a person of integrity. Integrity is the sum total of all our everyday choices. The more consistent we are with our everyday choices, the more integrity we have. Take the story of golfer Bobby Jones.

From 1923-1930, Bobby Jones won 13 major championships in golf. His record was unmatched until 1973 when it was finally broken by Jack Nicklaus. In a championship match that he was playing in, Jones drove the ball into the woods. As he was looking for the ball, he accidentally nudged it. Although no one saw him move the ball, he penalized himself one stroke (according to the rules), which caused him to lose the match by that margin. Afterward, when reporters praised him for his integrity, he responded that they might as well praise him and congratulate him for not robbing a bank.

In Martin Luther King's famous *I Have a Dream* speech, he talks about people being judged by the content of their character. The true measure of a person's character is what they would do if they knew that no one would ever find out. The West Point honor code states,

"A cadet will not lie, cheat, steal, or tolerate those who do."

Your integrity is the most valuable thing that you possess. Here is an older poem from Dale Wimbrow, entitled *The Man in the Glass* about your integrity and how ultimately, you know whether you have it or don't

The Man in the Glass
When you get what you want in your struggle for self
and the world makes you king for a day.
Just go to the mirror and look at yourself
And see what that man has to say.

For it isn't your father or mother or wife
Whose judgement upon you must pass,
The fellow whose verdict counts most in your life
Is the one staring back from the glass.

You may be like Jack Horner and chisel a plum
And think you're a wonderful guy,
But the man in the glass says you're only a bum
If you can't look him straight in the eyes.

He's the fellow to please -- never mind all the rest,
For he's with you clear to the end;
And you've passed your most dangerous, difficult test
If the man in the glass is your friend.

You may fool the whole world down the pathway of years
And get pats on the back as you pass,
But your final reward will be heartache and tears
If you've cheated the man in the glass"

POSITIVE ATTITUDE

The cliché goes that your attitude determines your altitude. This is true more often than not. Your outlook on life determines much of your success. Positive people are positive because they choose to be. It is often said that whether you think you can or can't, you are probably right. Every action – big or small – begins as a thought. Having positive thoughts will lead to a positive attitude which will lead to positive actions. Being positive does not mean ignoring the negative. Being positive means overcoming the negative. This reminds me of the great Italian violinist Niccolo Paganini when he encountered a difficulty at one of his concerts.

Paganini was playing a difficult piece of music before a large audience. Suddenly one string on his violin snapped, yet he continued to play, improvising beautifully. Then two more strings broke, and he completed the song playing with only one string. The crowd applauded wildly when he finished. However, he wasn't finished. He proceeded to play an encore with only one string.

Paganini didn't let something that seemed to be a deal-breaker interfere with his attitude and outlook on what he needed to do. The violinist was supposed to play and that is what he was going to do – and do it to the best of his ability. When it comes to life, we truly are about as happy as we decide we will be. It is up to us to determine our attitude. No situation - or person can make us feel a certain way unless we allow it. Life is less about what happens to us and more about how we react to the stuff that happens to us.

We are in charge of our actions and our attitude. We can't control whether we are faced with having only one-string, but we can certainly decide how we will play that one-string. This is similar to what the great philosopher and scholar Captain Jack Sparrow said in *The Pirates of the Caribbean* when he remarked, "The problem is not the problem. The problem is our attitude toward the problem."

If you have a positive mindset and optimistic outlook on life, you can achieve just about anything. This attitude can also rub off on others. Enthusiasm is contagious. Mark Twain wrote about enthusiasm and turning a negative into a positive in his book *The Adventures of Tom Sawyer* when he talked about Tom getting in trouble and having to paint the fence. He acted as if he was having so much fun that he tricked his friends into not only painting the fence for him but paying him to do so. That was definitely an early case of enthusiasm being contagious. Jon Gordon, a leadership expert and author of many best-sellers agrees strongly with the power of positivity as he says,

> "The great thing about positivity is that it never decreases when you share it. When you share positivity with others it grows and expands in their lives and yours."

DISCIPLINE

A good definition of discipline is doing what has to be done; when it has to be done; as well as you can possibly do it, and then doing it that way all of the time. Having the discipline to do what you are supposed to do is hard work but is worth it in the long run. Self-discipline is a matter of how hard you are willing to work when no one is watching. Self-discipline is not the path to instant gratification. The reward is much farther down the road, and not always obvious. Do the next right thing whether anyone is looking or whether or not you'll be rewarded for it.

Discipline gets you out of bed in the morning. Discipline reminds you of your goals. Discipline wants you to do what you don't want to do so that you can accomplish what you want to accomplish. Discipline helps you to stay focused and build mental toughness because it helps you develop daily habits. It helps you develop repetition so that success becomes automatic.

Here is a quick story from Pat Williams in his book *Be Like Mike*,

> "Once I asked Michael (Jordan) what he was thinking about when he took the final shot in Game Six in 1998," said Jordan's business partner and Washington Capitals owner Ted Leonsis. "Michael said, "I wasn't thinking about anything because I'd taken that shot a million times in practice. If I hadn't taken that shot a million times, then I would have had something to think about."

During Navy Seals training, they emphasize intense and extreme training so that your actions become automatic. They believe that when you are under pressure, you don't rise to the occasion, you sink to the level of your training. Hockey's greatest player ever, Wayne Gretzky echoed the Navy Seals philosophy when he said,

> "No matter who you are, no matter how good an athlete you are, we're creatures of habit. The better your habits are, the better they'll be in pressure situations."

Jerry West is one of the all-time great basketball players who played for the Los Angeles Lakers. In fact, his dribbling silhouette is what is used as the NBA's official logo. You don't get to be representative of the NBA and respected worldwide if you take too many days off or are unreliable. In fact, West once said,

> "You can't get much done in life if you only work on days that you feel good."

One would wonder if Baseball Hall of Famer Cal Ripken, Jr. saw that quote when he was younger because Ripken became the textbook example of dependability. The Baltimore Orioles' iron man played in 2,632 straight games spanning more than 16 years. This record broke the 56 year old mark held by Lou Gehrig. Ripken went on to be inducted into baseball's Hall of Fame in his first year of eligibility on January 9, 2007. He probably had some days that he didn't feel good but he pressed on. He was already talented but his dependability took his game to the highest level.

Mediocre players are the ones always pointing out the times they do something good. However, good players expect to perform certain tasks over and over again routinely. Good players remember the times that they fail to do something. Consistency involves good habits. It involves a sense of dependability. Dependability is the ability to be relied upon. It is not only about being there physically but being there at your best. It is about loyalty and commitment, about being someone on whom your teammates can count on. To be this kind of teammate, you need to develop discipline.

RESPONSIBILITY

If you develop the habits of success, you'll make success a habit. These habits lead to being a responsible person. The legendary Tennessee Women's Basketball Coach Pat Summitt described responsibility equaling accountability equaling ownership, meaning that those words were synonymous and necessary. She said that a sense of ownership is the most powerful weapon a team or organization can have.

Every person has control over their choices and their behaviors. Responsible athletes own their choices and actions. They don't look for excuses. In fact, think for a minute as to what is in the middle of excuses? The answer is "u". You make hundreds of choices daily. Those choices are solely yours. It is not the coach's fault that you didn't put forth the effort, were selfish or had a bad attitude. As the old saying goes, excuses don't exist on great teams – it was raining for both teams.

One of Abraham Lincoln's favorite stories to tell was that of a man who killed both of his parents. When that man's trial came and he had to take the witness stand, he argued for mercy because he was an orphan. Take responsibility for your actions. This also reminds me of the story of two brothers whose lives took completely different paths. One became a successful businessman; the other, a homeless alcoholic.

A newspaper reporter asked the homeless brother why his life had turned out as it had. The downtrodden brother complained that his father had been a drunk and verbally abused them growing up. After this, the reporter went to the successful brother and asked the same question. The thriving sibling responded enthusiastically that he had been motivated to make a better life because of his father's drunken, abusive tirades. One of those brothers let the circumstances of his life hold him back. The other had used those same circumstances as the fuel to propel him toward success.

These two brothers experienced the same set of circumstances but made two different choices. How often do we blame others for our present situation? As an athletic director, I once had an athlete that got arrested for shoplifting and was subsequently suspended per the school's written policies. The parents and the athlete were upset and used any excuse that they could think of. However, they never once said that she didn't steal the items. They admitted that she stole the items, they just didn't want any consequences. You are free to make choices but you are not free from the consequences of those decisions.

Coach Mike Krzyzewski at Duke likes to talk about collective responsibility. If you are in a sinking boat, you should not be glad that the hole isn't on your end of the boat. In the end, the hole at the other end of the boat is going to end up sinking everybody. With collective responsibility, we are all accountable to each other. When a player hits a double, that is our double. When a player scores a touchdown, that is our touchdown. When a player misses a shot, that is our miss. Collectively, as a team, we are responsible to one another. You are your brother's keeper. What one teammate does affects everybody. What you do affects others.

In the 1997 NBA Finals, Michael Jordan was sick with a stomach virus. There was concern that he might not play in Game 5 against the Utah Jazz. However, it was a big game and his teammates were relying on him. Jordan would not disappoint as he was committed to winning his 5th championship that year. Jordan scored 38 points that night playing 44 of the 48 possible minutes.

The effort he came out and showed us was incredible. He's not only the greatest player ever, but he's the greatest leader ever." It is probably not likely that the Bulls would have won that game that night against Hall of Famers Karl Malone and John Stockton. A loss might have swung the momentum in the Jazz's favor and ultimately cost the Bulls their championship.

Michael felt an obligation and a responsibility to his team. He was committed to his team. But his commitment began years earlier. If he hadn't made daily decisions in the years leading up to this game, he wouldn't have had the strength of conviction to sacrifice as much as he did physically that night. He wouldn't have had the mental toughness of a champion. This reminds me of another story of commitment that Kevin

Templeton tells about in his book *To The Hilt*,

> Hernando Cortez was a Spanish conquistador who went to Mexico in 1519. Cortez had six hundred soldiers and eleven ships. He introduced horses to a new continent. Many other conquerors with superior resources had attempted to colonize the Yucatan Peninsula without success. The powerful Aztecs ruled the central valley of Mexico with a mighty empire that plundered weaker tribes and hoarded vast amounts of gold, silver, and jewelry. The Aztecs were feared and hated by the other tribes. Cortez needed a way to energize and motivate his men.
>
> After landing, Cortez's men were probably more than a little fearful and nervous about the unknown challenges they might face in this new land. The men expected their leader to inspire and reassure them that their mission would be a success. Visions of riches no doubt danced in their heads. They were eager to hear Cortez's instructions. The first thing Cortez told the men was, "Burn the boats. All of them."
>
> Would you have done that? Not me! I'd keep one ship just in case the enemies were too tough. The Spaniards had gunpowder weapons, but what if the Aztecs had lasers? What if there were monsters/dinosaurs/zombies/diseases that were too numerous or difficult to deal with? Hey, the unknown can be a very frightening prospect. Cortez answered his crew's fears and maybe his own doubts by burning all the ships. It was his way of pushing all his chips into the center of the table. They were all-in. They were committed to the mission and to each other. They would be wildly successful or die in the attempt. We could say Cortez lived to the hilt. Defeat was never an option.

Kevin Templeton pretty much summed up commitment and taking true ownership in what you are doing. If you are on a team, then you should be all-in with your training and your coachability.

RESPECT

Respect is essentially being selfless and valuing others. Having humility doesn't mean that you think less of yourself, rather that it means you think of yourself less. Think about when you have a conversation with a person – are you listening so that you can understand what they are saying or are you listening with the intent to reply?

Dale Carnegie wrote one of the most read books of all-time called *How to Make Friends and Influence People*. He summed up how we should deal with others when he said,

> "There is one all-important law of human conduct. If we obey that law, we shall almost never get into trouble. In fact, that law, if obeyed, will bring us countless friends and constant happiness. But the very instant we break the law, we shall get into endless trouble. The law is this: Always make the other person feel important."

No matter who you are working with or interacting with, respect is important. We are all in this together whether it as teammates or in everyday life. Everybody has value as a person. Jesse Jackson, the famous civil rights activist once said, "Never look down on anybody unless you're helping them up."

You should be treating people the way that you want to be treated. Everybody has a story. We can learn something from everybody that we meet. Treat everyone with kindness, not necessarily because they are kindhearted but because you are. Instead of judging people by their past, help them to create a positive future.

Do you thank your teachers for their hard work and sacrifice? Do you publicly applaud your teammates when they do something that largely goes unnoticed? Do you put your lunch tray away so that the lunch lady doesn't have to? Do you greet the custodian with a smile and a hello? In fact, do you know the custodian's name that keeps your school from being a messy heap of trash? Do you make eye contact with people that are talking with you? Do you respect your coach's game plan?

We have differences as people. We listen to different music, we have different backgrounds, we grew up in different cultures, we have different preferences and we even have different opinions. That doesn't make us right and someone else wrong. It just makes us different. If you are going to maximize your potential for success in life, you have to understand how to work with others and respect others.

Usain Bolt is one of the most accomplished track athletes ever. He was the first person to ever hold the world record in the 100 meter and 200 meter sprints at the same time. After winning a race at the 2012 Olympics, the Jamaican-born Bolt was being interviewed on television when he stopped the interview to stand at attention while the U.S. national anthem was being played as Sanya Richards-Ross was on the medal stand for winning the women's 400 meter race. This was an impressive sign of respect and sportsmanship.

Sportsmanship and respect is a great opportunity to demonstrate to the world what kind of person we are. It is a reflection of our character as much as it is the other person. Consider the example from a NCAA softball game.

In May of 2008, Western Oregon and Central Washington were playing a softball game that could determine which team went to the NCAA Division II playoffs. In the second inning, Western Oregon's Sara Tucholsky hit a home run. This was the senior's first-ever home run. In her excitement, she didn't touch first base and when she turned to go back, her knee buckled and she went down. She was in such pain that she couldn't continue running the bases.

Her team was told, however, that if any of the players or staff tried to help her around the bases, that Sara would be ruled out. If they sent in a pinch-runner then the home run wouldn't count and it would just be a single.

Central Washington's Mallory Holtman and teammate Liz Wallace proceeded to pick up Sara and carried her. As they approached each base, they carefully helped her touch each base. Like the injured Tucholsky, Holtman was a senior but unlike Tucholsky, she had hit many home runs in her career. In fact, she was Central Washington's all-time leader. Holtman and Wallace's sportsmanlike act allowed Tucholsky to earn her first home run ever. It is also contributed to their own team losing that game and not going to the playoffs.

Holtman's Central Washington teammates agreed with her that it was the right thing to do. In fact, the crowd even gave them a standing ovation as they crossed home plate. That was the ultimate form of respect for another person and respect for the game.

GROWTH

Leaders are learners. If you want to maximize your potential then you must continue to grow. The University of Michigan football coach Jim Harbaugh likes to say that his team is trying to be better today than they were yesterday and be better tomorrow than they are today. There is no such thing as staying the same. You are either getting better or getting worse. Change is inevitable but growth is optional. You get to choose whether you want to improve or slide backwards.

Are you coachable? Are you open to correction? We can learn something from everyone that we meet and from every situation that we are in. It has been said that wise men learn from other men's failures but fools learn only by their own failures. Do you learn by watching others? When you are on the bench do you clown around or do you pay attention? We might already have experienced a lot of success in life but we can still continue to grow. As John Wooden said,

"It is what you learn after you know it all that counts."

As humans, we don't like change and we don't like growth because it takes work and is sometimes painful. However, if there is no irritation or effort, then it is difficult for growth to take place.

Consider how we get a valuable pearl. It is because of irritation that leads to something special. A grain of sand or some other small object slips into the shell of the oyster. Because of the irritating nature of the sand, the oyster releases some fluid (I think of it like when we get something in our eye and our eye waters) and surrounds the irritant, eventually encapsulating it in layers of secretion.

Thus, we end up with a beautiful round pearl that was started by some irritant. Through our challenges and experiences – and through others' challenges and experiences – valuable lessons can be learned and growth can be realized.

Many of us do not honestly evaluate ourselves. We make a basket or get a hit and we think everything is okay and don't continually strive to get better. Did we get lucky? Was our competition weak? You should be in a constant mindset of trying to improve yourself so that your team can improve. How do you evaluate yourself? It is said that we judge ourselves based on our intentions but we judge others based on their actions. Also, are you honest with your assessments about yourself? If you are not playing as much as you'd like, do you blame your coach (or the politics involved)? If a game is lost, do you blame others (officials, coach, other players, etc...)? What if you didn't even play. It can't be your fault, right?

That reminds me of a story about a coach that I knew. "Coach B" was always talking to his basketball teams about turnovers. They would often discuss whether it was the passer or the receiver's fault on various turnovers. One day during a game, there was a turnover off of a pass. He leaned forward on the bench and asked a couple of his reserves who was at fault for that last turnover? One of them said the passer and one of them said the receiver. He paused for a moment and then yelled, "Wrong! It's your fault. You haven't worked on your game and haven't improved enough so I have to play those guys out there."

That story might be a little harsh but it does make you think. Coaches typically want to play the players that give them the best chance of winning. If coaches lose, it might cost them their jobs. But at the very least, losses cause coaches all kinds of frustrations and headaches. They are competitors, also and don't like to lose. They want to play the players that give them the best chance to win. This doesn't mean a basketball coach will always put out the five most talented players on the floor, but they will try to put the right five players on the floor that fit and work together best. If you are not out there, then you need to honestly evaluate why. Unfortunately, too many athletes take an approach that I saw played out in an unexpected way on the television show, *Shark Tank*.

The rich investors were pitched an idea called "The Skinny Mirror". The concept of this mirror was to make a person feel better about what they look like. However, a flaw in its concept was that the mirror was not an accurate reflection. The Skinny Mirror would be placed in dressing rooms of clothing stores. Customers would try on the clothes and like what they saw in the reflection. They would then buy the clothes because they felt good about how the clothes make them look. The reality is that the mirror did not change the person. It just merely communicated a false reality to them.

If the only feedback that you are wanting to listen to is that of people not willing to tell you the truth, then you will struggle to maximize your potential. If you only want to hear positive things about you then you will fall short in the growth department. Just because a friend tells you that you should be starting because you are really good, doesn't mean that the friend is correct. Your coach is probably a more accurate mirror than friends or family unless they are willing to hold you accountable for those things that you need to improve upon. At the end of the day, the best way to improve the team is to improve yourself. The best way to improve yourself is to put your pride and ego aside (The Skinny Mirror) aside and look at yourself objectively.

3.
LEADERSHIP
DEFINED

"I alone cannot change the world, but I can cast a stone across the waters to create many ripples."
– Mother Teresa

"Leadership is not about positions, titles or flowcharts but about one life influencing another."
– John C. Maxwell

"Every individual exerts some influence, either for good or evil, upon others."
– Henry Ward Beecher

"People often call me an overachiever, but I'm not an overachiever. I'm an overbeliever."
– Dabo Swinney

"Leadership is about making others better as a result of your presence and making sure that this impact lasts in your absence."
– Harvard Business School

What are the qualities of a leader? If you are like most people, you will say "respect", "hard-working", "responsible", "trustworthy", "reliable", "coachable", "enthusiastic", or "encouraging". None of these words are specific to your role as a star, reserve, upperclassman, freshman or captain. Any player can possess these qualities. They are not exclusive to a captain.

John C. Maxwell has written more than 100 books on leadership. He is considered the foremost expert on leadership. He has had a profound impact on my view of leadership. What has shaped my thinking the most has been his definition of leadership in which he says,

> "Leadership is not about titles, positions or flowcharts, but about one life influencing another."

No matter what your current position is, you have the opportunity to lead because you can influence somebody. Maxwell is also famous for saying that,

> "A leader knows the way, shows the way and goes the way."

Once again, this is not exclusive to captains or upperclassmen. Anyone on a team can be a leader according to these definitions by Maxwell.

LEADERSHIP IS INFLUENCE

Many people mistakenly think that leadership is a title. Titles may give a person some prestige or artificial power, but true leadership involves the amount of influence that a person has. Maxwell further states that a leader without followers is just a person going for a long walk.

Great leaders are influential. People want to follow great leaders. You don't have to have a title to be influential. People are willing to be led and influenced by others if they feel that the leader can take them where they want to go.

Your team captain, your boss, your political representative may not be a strong leader because they aren't influential. They may have perceived power because of their title but they are lacking in the influence area. They might not have the charisma or the character or the results that people are looking for. They might not connect with others.

What does all of this mean for you? Some of you reading this do not have a title. Some of you may feel that you are not important. However, everyone has the ability to influence someone. You have the ability to make positive choices. You have the ability to be enthusiastic. You have the ability to be trustworthy. Essentially, you have the ability to be a person of character that others believe in.

If you are one of the harder workers on a team and you are successful, that will speak loudly. If you add value to people's lives, they will be indebted to you. If others know that you truly care about them, they will be loyal to you.

The world around us needs strong leadership now more than ever. You may not be THE leader, THE boss or THE captain but you can be a leader. Everyone has a scope of influence. At the very least, you can influence yourself.

THE TEAM WON'T LISTEN TO ME

In one of the Student-Athlete Leadership Team training sessions that I was conducting, a student asked a question that had the rest of the group nodding in agreement and adding their two-cents worth to the conversation.

"How do I get my teammates to listen to me?" There are many variations to this question, but they all come down to student-athletes wanting to influence their teammates in some way. John C. Maxwell, considered by many to be the foremost leadership expert in the world, teaches that leadership is influence.

Sometimes we look at our team and see the negatives. We want everyone to respect us and follow us. This may not always be possible. Don't worry about everyone. Worry about those that you can influence.

Any player on a team probably has 2 or 3 close friends on that team. Those are the people that you should focus on leading and influencing. If they are not willing to follow you and do the positive things that you are doing, then you need to analyze why not? There are only two reasons a close friend will not follow you: (1) they don't respect you; (2) you have the wrong close friends.

Leadership is influence. Nothing more, nothing less. However, the absolute first person you influence is yourself. You should be doing the right things. Your character should be strong. If a friend doesn't respect you enough to follow your example or words, then you need to make yourself more respectable. Be a person worthy of having followers.

If you are worthy of respect, are walking the walk and talking the talk, but your close friends still aren't willing to follow your lead, then you need to analyze who your "close" friends are. If your character is strong and you have the right personality, then why wouldn't your friend want to follow your lead? Be careful of these people. There are two types of people in your life: those that make you better and those that don't.

If you are leading yourself correctly and have the right people around you, then focus on influencing them. What you'll find is that there will now be 3, 4 or 5 people that are influenced in the right way and are doing what is needed for your team to experience success.

Now imagine if one of those friends you influenced has a close friend that you don't have a strong connection with? You can't influence that other person but your friend can. You helped influence your friend so indirectly you have helped influence this other person.

To influence someone, you must have a strong connection. You can't reach everyone but you can lead yourself first and then influence those that you have a good relationship with. Through your good influence on a few, then it can possibly multiply to the whole team.

Don't worry about what you can't control. Don't worry about the teammates that you don't have a strong connection with. Worry about leading yourself and influencing those nearest to you.

TWO TYPES OF LEADERS

When I was in high school, I was in Band class but I didn't enjoy being in the class. My attitude was bad and my actions reflected that. I was 1st trumpet and my friend was 2nd trumpet. If you are not aware, trumpets are loud and carry much of the melody. Every instrument is crucial, but a trumpet can certainly take center stage.

My friend and I decided to make up a game to alleviate some of our boredom. We came up with a point system, where we accumulated points based on screwing up. For instance, if we messed up and got the teacher to stop and start the song over, then we got so-many points. If we got a dirty look, we got so-many points. If we were publicly reprimanded, then we got so-many points. If we got an eraser thrown at us, we got so many points. You get the picture.

Well, one-day I was doing a great job – meaning, I was doing a bad job and screwing up a lot. Finally, the band teacher had enough. He stopped the song and then proceeded to calmly tell me "Jamy, there are two types of people in this world. Those who lead us forward and those who lead us backwards, and you lead us backwards. NOW GET OUT!"

Boy was I excited. All the previous points I had accumulated that day didn't matter. I had just gotten kicked out of class. I won the day automatically!

Even though I was young and thought I was cool, that story has stuck with me all these years. My band teacher was right. We are all leaders but it is just a matter of whether or not we are leading people forward or backwards.

We make choices every day as to whether we will use our influence positively or negatively. And make no mistake, we all have influence. I had an influence on the 2nd chair trumpet, which also increased my influence over the entire band, which meant that I had an influence on whether the song sounded good or not.

SENIOR NOT VOTED CAPTAIN

When I became the head coach at a college in the southern part of the country, I decided to have the team vote for captains. There were 22 players (including varsity and junior varsity). Each player would be allowed to cast a vote for the two players that they felt were the best candidates to be the captain that year.

We had a senior that was also the starting point guard. Essentially, she played the position that is generally thought of as the quarterback or the leader on the floor. The point guard runs the offense and is supposed to get everyone into the correct spots. When the votes were tallied, this senior who was the incumbent starting point guard received exactly one vote – her own.

After the results were announced and the captains were set, she came up to me and said, "Coach, if you just let me be captain, then I will be a leader. I will show you what I can do. I will show my teammates what I can do."

This player did not understand true leadership. She was already a leader but in a negative way. Fortunately, her teammates recognized this. After being in the program for three years, she had already demonstrated her leadership by failing to influence teammates for the better. She fell into a common trap. She equated positional leadership with influence. If only she could be a captain, then she would have influence. But this player already had influence with at least one or two players and the team had seen how she had squandered that opportunity to help move them forward.

THE BUTTERFLY EFFECT

One person can have such a strong effect on the world such as Martin Luther King, Bill Gates, Steve Jobs, Michael Jordan, and Mother Teresa. In the same way, one player can have a strong influence on a team. You never know what kind of result your actions can have. You might not be able to do everything but you can do something. Your something might be just what is needed to begin changing things for the better. Gandhi said, "Be the change you want to see in the world." There is no telling what can be accomplished when you decide to use your influence in a positive way.

It is like the butterfly effect, which was first theorized by Edwin Lorenz in 1963 to help explain weather patterns and chaos theory. It states that one small change can result in a large change later on. For instance, a tornado in Texas might have been caused by a series of weather events that all started off with a butterfly flapping its' wings in a Brazilian rain forest. The butterfly didn't power the tornado. The flapping of its wings was just the beginning of a chain reaction.

One thing happened which leads to another thing happening which leads to another thing happening. If the butterfly hadn't flapped its' wings at that exact time then the weather system might have been different. Here is one such example that Larry Gallegos points out on his Mortgage Cicerone blog. This story highlights of a chain reaction of events that changed history,

> One day in the countryside of Scotland, a common and poor farmer was toiling in his field when suddenly he heard a cry for help. Startled, he recognized someone was in trouble and the plea was coming from a nearby bog. Immediately he dropped what he was doing and ran to the source of the plea. When he located the voice calling for help, he stumbled upon a terrified boy up to his waist in black muck,

screaming and sinking deeper and deeper into the bog as each minute passed.

The farmer calmly retrieved ropes from nearby, pulled the boy out of the bog and saved his life.

The next day, an elegantly dressed nobleman arrived at the farmers small and simple home. When the nobleman stepped out of his carriage, he introduced himself as the father of the boy the farmer had saved.

Emotionally, the nobleman thanked the farmer and asked to repay the farmer for saving his son's life. The farmer waved off the offer and informed the nobleman he could not accept payment for doing what was right.

At that moment, the nobleman asked if the farmer had a son in which the farmer replied he did. Subsequently, the nobleman insisted he provide the farmer's son an education on par with that he would provide his own son. Upon leaving the farmers house, the nobleman told the farmer, "if the lad is anything like his father, he'll no doubt grow to be a man we both will be proud of."

The nobleman's prediction concerning the farmer's son proved to be prophetic.

True to the nobleman's word, the farmer's son attended the best schools in the world and eventually graduated from St. Mary's Hospital Medical School in London. More importantly, he went on to become known throughout the world as the noted Sir Alexander Fleming, the discoverer of Penicillin.

Years afterward, the same nobleman's son who was saved from the bog was stricken with pneumonia.

What saved his life this time? Penicillin.

The name of the nobleman? Lord Randolph Churchill
.

His son's name? Sir Winston Churchill, the great British Prime Minister who saved England from being taken over by Nazi Germany and Adolph Hitler.

Small things can make a difference. Everything that we do matters. A well-place smile or much needed encouraging word might brighten someone's day to the extent that they treat someone else better. We can make a difference in the world and on our teams just by being the change agent and starting a chain reaction of positivity.

LESSON OF THE GEESE

When you are looking at having the best team possible and being the best teammate you can be, then it might help to consider some lessons that geese can teach us. Yes, that is right, I said geese! Consider the following items about geese,

As each goose flaps its wings, it creates an uplift for the bird behind it. By flying in a V-formation, the whole flock adds 71 percent more flying range than if each bird flew alone. The lesson we can learn is that teammates who share a common direction and sense of community can get where they are going quicker and easier when they are bringing each other along and using each other's momentum and sharing energy.

When a goose gets sick, wounded, or shot down, two geese drop out of formation and follow it down. They stay with the goose to help and protect it until it is able to fly again or dies. Then they launch out with another formation to catch up with the flock. The lesson for our team is to stick by one another and build each other up. Help each other because we can do more together than by ourselves. We are vulnerable by ourselves.

Whenever a goose falls out of the formation, it suddenly feels the drag and resistance of trying to fly alone and quickly gets back into formation to take advantage of the lifting power of the bird in front. The lesson for us is to not try to go it alone. It is easier with teammates.

When the lead goose gets tired, it rotates back into the formation and another goose flies at the point position. We can learn from this and understand that we can all be leaders at some point. We can all take turns doing the hard tasks and sharing leadership.

The geese in formation honk from behind to encourage those up front to keep up their speed. We need to make sure our honking from behind is encouraging and not something that is less than helpful.

This might seem a little silly to look at geese for leadership inspiration, but these are very good points that we can apply to ourselves and our team. I also guarantee you that the next time you hear honking up in the sky and see geese flying by, you'll look at them differently.

CHAUNCEY BILLUPS

How would you handle yourself if people were calling you a failure? How would you react if you were in a situation where you weren't successful? Would you feel that you couldn't lead? Chauncey Billups was the third pick in the 1997 NBA draft. He appeared to be a bust early on in his career. In fact, he was traded five times and dealt with some various injuries.

However, through it all, he kept his focus on being the best he could be and adding value to his teammates. He didn't play the victim card or wallow in self-pity. His career had it all from lottery pick to draft bust to role player to champion with the Detroit Pistons. In an interview with MLive, former NBA player O.J. Mayo said that Billups was the best leader.

"Chauncey Billups, in my mind, is the best leader in our league. Chris Paul is a great point guard. Deron Williams is great. Rajon Rondo. But Chauncey Billups is by far the No. 1 leader in our league. Just being around him and seeing how he leads on and off the court was a big thing."

In a 2012 *Grantland.com* article, former NBA coach Sam Mitchell said,

> "Do you know how hard it is for players to look themselves in the mirror and say, 'It's me and not everybody else' and start changing?" "It's a difficult thing to do. And then when people are calling you a bust and you're the third pick of the draft? And to deal with those labels and to overcome them? It don't happen."

In that same article, Billups reflected on his own growth,

> "The thing that saved me was being honest with myself and saying it's not the coach's fault or the team's fault that I'm not playing. I'm just not ready and I have to look in the mirror and ask myself, 'All right, what do I have to do?'"

Billups was a great example of rising up and having a positive influence regardless of his role or situation. His consistent attitude of leadership was stronger than any environment or situation he would face.

UCONN WBB

The UCONN women's basketball team has been one of the greatest sports dynasties since Geno Auriemma took over as the coach in 1985. As of the 2016-17 season, they have won a record 11 NCAA National Championships and have the two longest winning streaks in NCAA Division I women's college basketball history with 111 and another with 91 straight wins. They have been good for a long time.

One of the reasons is that they have developed a culture whereby the players hold each other accountable. They also take ownership in the recruiting process as well. Such sustained success has been nurtured by so many players from the past that bought in to the culture and then passed it on to the next generation. Here are a couple of 1990's examples from John Walters book *The Same River Twice* that could be just as true today but with different player's names substituted in,

> Shea Ralph was USA Player of the Year and someone from USA Today was interviewing her, and they asked her why she chose Connecticut. She told them, "Well, Coach Auriemma was the only coach that told me if I was really good I'd play a lot, and if I sucked I wasn't playing."

> ...In her locker, Swin Cash taped a picture of herself crying on the bench after a loss to Iowa State in the NCAA tournament the season before ('98-'99). I asked her why she has the picture up there. She says to me, "I don't want to ever feel that way again. I don't want to ever forget what that felt like. Look at me. I look pathetic."

> ...When Diana Taurasi visited the campus, Shea Ralph took her around. Dee was just so impressed with Shea, how tough she is, how nice she is, how loyal she is. Shea tells her playing at UCONN was the best decision she made in her life. "But it's not going to be easy", she warns Dee. Dee already knows that. That's why she comes. She isn't looking for something easy. It had already been too easy for too long. Everything she does is perfect. She can score at will. Nobody ever challenges her, on or off the court. It's far too much of, "Whatever you want, Diana. You're the best, Diana."

> ...A lot of players will look at our roster, see all our talent and say, "there's no room for me there." Diana Taurassi sees a roster that has Sue Bird, Swin Cash, Shea Ralph, Svetlana Abrosimova, and Ashjha Jones on it and says, "That's where I want to be. I want to play with the best. I want to be the best."

A team's culture is ultimately determined by the players and their actions. Those were just three examples of UConn players that held themselves and their teammates to a higher standard. They expected more out of themselves. Fast forwarding a decade or more and Mechelle Voepel on ESPN.com in 2017 wrote that UCONN's culture is maintained by the players both past and present.

> The Huskies play at a level that seems closer to the WNBA than to college ball. We've lauded the members of the coaching staff a lot, and they deserve it. Auriemma is as good as it gets.

> But even he would say that the players should be credited for how they buy into the system and enforce it themselves.

> Among the biggest complaints, you'll hear from women's basketball coaches nationwide is that while players are more athletic than ever, fundamentals have slipped. Specifically, shooting and passing on offense, and positioning and discipline on defense.

> There's also a familiar gripe that club basketball has eroded not just those fundamentals, but also a general sense of competitiveness: Kids play too many games of no consequence, except to show off their skills.

> Yet what are the hallmarks of UConn women's hoops? Great passing. High-percentage shooting. Not fouling on defense. Playing hard no matter what the score or how much time is left.

> Auriemma demands these things, but the players do, too, by holding each other accountable. That continues into their professional careers.

> At an Olympic team training camp last year at UConn, Bird acknowledged that there were moments when she felt 18 again, trying to prove herself. Never mind that she was on her way to her fourth gold medal. That sense of obligation to a standard remained. As it will for the current Huskies

navigating their way to another milestone.

"You play every game the same way," Samuelson said. "Whether it's our first win, second win, 80th win -- whatever. We keep ourselves going without doubting things. We go into every game being confident."

Could these things be said of you? Do you reinforce the coach's values and philosophies when they are not around? Do you use lighter fluid or a fire extinguisher when faced with locker room fires? Furthermore, do you even try to prevent locker room fires? Are you jealous of others because you want the glory and the playing time or are you more interested in competition, which will take everyone to a higher level? Are you constantly creating a championship culture or one that focuses on individuals and personal agendas? Yes, UCONN might be talented but so are other teams. Their winning margin or differential is based upon their culture. They all buy into the team concept.

GEORGE BOIARDI

Every team has starters and a leading scorer, but most teams don't have players that influence teammates so much that they still celebrate that player and remember him years later. Some of the greatest stars are forgotten about soon after their playing days are finished. George Bioardi was a star player for the Cornell men's lacrosse team. He was also the captain.

More importantly, he was a player whose example on and off the field had a tremendous impact. He made his teammates better. He was the model leader. Unfortunately, on March 17, 2004, with just a couple of minutes remaining in a game, the defenseman threw himself into the path of a lacrosse ball to help out his goalie. The ball hit him in the chest and he would suffer a fatal injury.

Not only have there been star players and captains that have been long forgotten through the passage of time, sadly there have been athletes that have died while in the prime of their lives. Many of these athletes were remembered for a little while. Very few have ever been remembered as much as George Bioardi.

It was how he lived that has been so lasting in death. In fact, author Jon Gordon wrote a book entitled Hard Hat that pays homage to the legacy of George. All the profits from that book go to the George Bioardi foundation, which was founded by Ian Rosenberg, Dave Coors, and Billy Fort, to raise money for charitable organizations and events that were near and dear to Bioardi.

In addition, shortly before his death, Boiardi started the Big Red Readers program that had Cornell players going to read to local elementary school students. This still goes on today, as does the "21 Run", a 5K charity run organized by the lacrosse team. That is a legacy. That is influence.

Julie Greco wrote an article for Cornell's alumni magazine ten years after Boiardi's death highlighting how much his legacy still lives on. Here are a few of the notable passages that shed light on what true leadership and legacy are all about.

> For members of Big Red lacrosse, there is no last name necessary when speaking of "George." His name has become synonymous with hard work, dedication, humility, and selflessness. The team prides itself on winning the midfield battle each game and having an edge in what they refer to as "Boiardi stats" -- the ground balls, the hustle plays, the dirty work on which a game can usually turn. More than anything, the team wants to protect "George's House," something it has done with great regularity, going 64-13 (.831) on Schoellkopf Field since March 17, 2004.

> ...While the Class of 2007 was the last to have played with Boiardi, his legacy lives on in the locker room, with each freshman class learning about the athlete who wore No. 21 -- through a 21-minute-long video created by his former teammates to inspire future Big Red players.

> ...One of the players profoundly inspired by Boiardi and the way he lived his life was Tewaaraton Trophy winner Rob Pannell '13.

> ..."When working out, instead of doing 15 or 20 reps, I do 21. Instead of running 15- or 20-second sprints I run 21-second sprints," Pannell says. "Every time I see the number

'21,' I think of George Boiardi. 21 is not a number, it is a way of life ... Without 21, Cornell lacrosse is not Cornell lacrosse and I am not who I am. George Boiardi, with the help of the past Cornell lacrosse coaches, players and friends who knew him, shapes the young men that are Cornell lacrosse.

..."According to the record books, I hold the Cornell lacrosse assist record. The real truth is that George Boiardi does. George Boiardi has gotten an assist on every single practice, weight session, film session, goal, assist and win since his freshman year at Cornell."

..."I grew up with George, and I had the privilege of knowing him," Ian Rosenberger (co-founder of the Boiardi Foundation) says, "but to see how his ideals have carried on to guys who never even met him is just amazing to me. To hear guys like Max Seibald '09 and Rob Pannell '13, who never met him but are able to talk about George and really nail him to a tee, is really powerful. It's simply amazing to me to see how George has had a meaningful impact on so many lives."

Are you living a life of significance? Are you making the world a better place? If you left your team tomorrow what would your teammates say about you? What would future players on that team say about you? Would they even know your name? Players come and go. Stars come and go. Captains come and go. People who add value to others and make other people's lives better are remembered. They leave a lasting legacy. That is why we still talk about Martin Luther King, Gandhi, Nelson Mandela, and Mother Theresa. People who made a difference in the world. You can do this on your team but not if you feel entitled or believe that certain tasks are below you.

BEN ZOBRIST

When the star-laden Chicago Cubs won the 2016 World Series, they were led by an unlikely hero Ben Zobrist. Nobody would ever have thought that a guy from Olivet Nazarene University, a small NAIA school, would appear in three different World Series with three different teams, let alone be named the World Series MVP in 2016.

In 2015, the Kansas City Royals acquired Zobrist in mid-season and he quickly became a fan favorite with his ability to play multiple positions, his scrappy play, and his up-beat personality. He was a big part of the Royals winning the World Series that year. After the season, the Royals couldn't re-sign everyone and Zobrist went to join his former manager, Joe Maddon, with the Chicago Cubs. He had previously played for Maddon with the Tampa Bay Rays. In fact, they went all the way to the World Series in 2008. His reunion with Maddon would be the start of a magical run. The Chicago Cubs had not won a World Series title in 108 years. Zobrist would have a huge part in making that happen. He led the Cubs with 10 hits in the series, while batting .357. His double in the 10th inning drove in the game-winning run. He was named the series MVP.

Bill Chastain of MLB.com put together a story that praised Zobrist's leadership back in 2013 *BEFORE* he had even won his World Championships with the Royals and Cubs,

> "If you ask any manager in the league, they'd be like, 'This is a guy I want on my team,'" said manager Joe Maddon. "To be with him daily, you get to see it all and all the little things that he does, and beyond that, all the team things that he does. This guy is all about winning. That's it. That's it. He doesn't care about his batting average. He does only in the sense that if he's not hitting well, that means he's not helping the team. He's all about the team and he's really unique, and I don't even know where we would be without him."

> "[Ben is] somebody you really rely on and somebody you almost come to expect to be out there every day and give you everything he has," said teammate Matt Joyce. "He's obviously a leader off the field as well as on. As far as his beliefs and his morals and his values, I think they go a long way with providing some guidance to the younger guys. He's a great teammate."

34

An unheralded player with a background that was nothing special made it to the top of his profession because he had the proper team-first attitude. He constantly made himself better as a player and as a person, which made his teams better. He might not have been as talented as some other players but he worked harder and constantly modeled the right attitude. This led to increased respect from his teammates. Because of this, he was able to better influence his teams to achieve their potential.

CONTAGIOUS ENTHUSIASM

We rarely can control the situation but we can always control our attitudes. In his book *Winning Every Day*, the former Notre Dame football coach, Lou Holtz, tells the story of the Trappist monk who was allowed to say only two words every three years.

> After the first three years, he met with Brother Superior and said, "Bad bed!"
>
> Three years later, he came back to say, "Bad food!"
>
> After three more years of silence, the monk said, "No TV!"
>
> Another three years passed. This time, when the monk met with Brother Superior, he handed him his robes and sandals and announced, "I quit!"
>
> Brother Superior said, "Well don't expect me to try to dissuade you. You've done nothing but complain since you got here!"

It was pretty obvious that the monk didn't add value to his fellow monks or to the atmosphere. We all probably know at least one person in our lives that tend to be like the Trappist monk in the story. Always complaining or grumbling about something. It seems that they are not happy unless they are unhappy.

It would be easy for us to fall into the same trap and complain alongside this person but what does that solve? How does that make things better? Maybe you are like that Trappist monk. Maybe you are struggling with being positive.

In his book, *You Win In The Locker Room First,* author Jon Gordon shares with us research from two different studies. One from the HeartMath Institute and one from Harvard University. They essentially both support the notion that your body can physically affect other people up to 10 feet away. Your enthusiasm (or lack thereof) can literally be contagious. This applies to everyone, not just the captains. Each member of the team is contagious and every day you all are either sharing positive or negative energy with each other.

Championship cultures are built with positive contagious energy so it's essential that you share it. When you walk into the locker room, you have a decision to make: Are you going to be a germ or a big dose of vitamin C to your teammates? Will you infuse other people with positive energy or be an energy vampire and suck the life out of them?

If you are surrounded by negativity, then you can make the decision to smile a little more and while using kind words. Instead of being fixated on problems, you can focus on solutions. You have the power to make your surroundings a little more positive today.

4.
LEADING YOURSELF

"The most effective way to lead is to lead from within."
— Lolly Daskal

"Everyone thinks of changing the world, but no one thinks of changing himself."
— Leo Tolstoy

"Players who get bored in practice don't really want to be good. Champions get better. Losers get bored."
— Anonymous

"Champions never complain. They are too busy getting better."
— John Wooden

"Mastery of others is strength. Mastery of self is true power."
— Lao Tzu

"Coaches shouldn't have to push you to work hard, you should push yourself to work hard because you want to be a great player."
— Bobby Knight

"I am who I am today because of the choices I made yesterday."
— Eleanor Roosevelt

Sometimes the hardest person to lead is yourself. That is where everything starts. Remember what John C. Maxwell said about a leader knowing the way, showing the way and going the way? If you don't show and go the right way yourself then you will never experience the success that you are capable of achieving.

Strengthening your core values and your foundational principles that you learned about in chapter 2 are necessary for maximizing your potential and that of the team. You will make choices every day and so you need to know the way so that you can go the way. Sometimes the best leaders are those who follow. Wait, what?!? That's right. Remember leadership is just one person influencing another. Sometimes when you follow the directions of your coach, captain or a teammate – who are leading by example – you can then influence others to follow suit. But first, you have to do what's right and lead yourself.

YOU WILL NEVER PLAY VARSITY

When I went to college to play basketball, there was a sophomore on the team named Scottie Moore. Scottie had played on the junior varsity the year before. At the end-of-the-year evaluation meeting with the coach after his freshman year, he was told that he would never play varsity. He was too short, too slow and lacking varsity ability. In fact, he might not even make the JV if he came back.

That summer, Scottie dedicated himself to strengthening his game and his body. That next year, to the amazement of the coaches, he made the varsity. By the time, Scottie graduated he would finish his career as a 1,000 point scorer (remember he didn't play varsity as a freshman) and the 16th leading scorer in school history. Not bad for an out-of-shape 5'10" shooting guard who was told he probably wouldn't even make the team.

What a great story of someone that didn't quit and didn't play the victim card. When he didn't agree with his coach's assessment, he merely went out and worked harder on his game to prove the coach wrong. I don't remember him talking bad about the coaching staff during my time playing with him. He went about his business and continued to work to prove the doubters wrong. How about you? Will you be the kid that quits, transfers or criticizes the coach? Or will you be like Scottie Moore, that used it as motivation to achieve his maximum potential?

OPPORTUNITY KNOCKS

On January 12, 2015, the Ohio State Buckeyes won the inaugural College Football Playoffs when they defeated the explosive and exciting Oregon Ducks 42-20. It was impressive that the #1 and #2 teams squared off against each other in the Championship game. But maybe more impressive was the fact that both teams had prominent examples of players who took advantage of opportunities presented to them and didn't quit or become disruptive to their teams.

It is always difficult to see a student-athlete get disgruntled over playing time or their role on the team. Unfortunately, in most cases, the player quits. Oh, they might not physically quit the team but slowly and surely they cash out mentally. Instead of seeing the opportunity in every challenge, as the great British statesman Winston Churchill used to say, they see the difficulty in every opportunity. Unfortunately, instead of persevering, they make excuses and take on a victim-mentality.

Talk about preparing for an opportunity and being ready when it presents itself, one has to look no further than the guy that won the 2014 Heisman Trophy. Oregon's quarterback, Marcus Mariota earned the biggest award a college football player can receive. He was the best college football player in the nation that year but he didn't start for his high school team until his senior year.

Stop and think about that for a moment. The best player in all of college football didn't just become the best player overnight. He was very talented in high school but he didn't start. There was a quarterback starting ahead of him that would end up playing at the NCAA Division I level. Mariota kept working and preparing for his time. I believe Sir Winston Churchill or Abraham Lincoln would be proud of the way he didn't give up or fester a bad attitude. He waited patiently, prepared and then took advantage of his opportunity.

On the opposite sideline from Oregon in that first College Football Playoff Championship game was Ohio State who had a very interesting story at their quarterback position. Early in the 2014 season, the Buckeyes lost the Big 10's two-time offensive player of the year when quarterback Braxton Miller suffered an injury. That should have been the end of the Buckeyes championship hopes. Teams don't recover from losing a player that good, especially at the quarterback position. However, J.T. Barrett was ready. In fact, he was more than ready. All he did was dominate that year.

He would play so well during the regular season that he would finish 5th in the Heisman voting.

During the Michigan-Ohio State rivalry game on Thanksgiving Weekend, the game was close early in the fourth quarter and could go either way but then Barrett got hurt and had to leave the game. Barrett was the backup. Michigan fans had hope because they were thinking there was no way the backup to the backup could hurt them. They were wrong. Cardale Jones, Ohio State's third string quarterback at the start of the year, came in and orchestrated a convincing fourth quarter offensive display. Not only did he close the door on Michigan in relief but won his next three starts.

The third-stringer dominated Wisconsin in the Big 10 Championship Game, Alabama in the National Semi-Final Game and Oregon in the National Championship game. That season was his third year at Ohio State and he came into the season as the third string. He (and all Buckeye fans) are probably glad that he didn't quit or stop preparing. There was no way a third-string quarterback would ever be counted on to win a National Championship, right?!? But Jones continued to prepare and was ready for the opportunity.

When preparation meets opportunity, the possibility of success is enormous. Thomas Edison had it right when he said,

"Opportunity is missed by most people because it is dressed in overalls and looks like work."

That quote is just as appropriate today as when he was inventing the light bulb. We constantly choose our actions and attitudes. Think of how much college football history could be different if J.T. Barrett, Cardale Jones or Marcus Mariota had chosen to take the all-too familiar approach of complaining about their current situation instead of preparing for their future situation. They were ready to answer the door when opportunity knocked. What about you? Will you be ready for your opportunity when it comes?

PENALTY COSTS A TEAM THE GAME

During a NFL wildcard playoff game in January of 2016, two division rivals, the Pittsburgh Steelers and the Cincinnati Bengals faced off. The Bengals took a 16-15 lead with less than two minutes remaining in the game. The Steelers' star quarterback Ben Roethlisberger was hobbling around but was able to lead his team down the field. ON a 4th-and-3 play, he hit Antonio Brown for a completion at the 47 yard line. Bengals linebacker Vontaze Burfict was called for a 15-yard penalty on a malicious head-to-head hit on the reception. Antonio Brown would be knocked out of the game as a result of this hit.

This would put the Steelers' kicker Chris Boswell in range for a game-winning field goal, though the 50-yarder was no guarantee since his career long was 51 yards. There was also no guarantee that the Steelers would be able to get close enough with a very injured Roethlisberger and no Antonio Brown. None of this matter as the Bengals Adam "Pacman" Jones would enter the equation and provide late Christmas gift for the Steelers.

Jones completely lost his temper and went crazy on the officials. This would result in an additional 15-yard penalty and then give the Steelers an easy 35-yard field goal. All in all, the Steelers were awarded 30 free yards on their game-winning drive because of the lack of discipline and bone-headed plays by a couple of Bengals players.

Players get technical fouls or penalties all the time in sports but will almost always say they wouldn't do it when it matters most during crunch time. However, what you repeatedly do becomes who you are. These two players for the Bengals had a history of poor decisions. They did not have good habits and when it mattered most, they were not able to control themselves.

It has often been said that sports build character. Sports allow people to learn many lessons. The games themselves, though, don't necessarily build character. Instead, they reveal character. Just like a test that you might take in school doesn't build your knowledge base, but it reveals what you already know. The homework that you've done or not done is revealed when you take a test. In the same way, what you've done in practice and your workouts are revealed during the games. Your habits can make or break you. These two Bengals players failed to develop their daily habits. They failed to develop a strength of character that would allow them to stay focused on their goals.

To make matters worse, Jones had an explicit rant after the game blaming everybody but himself. His lack of responsibility further proved that he was in the wrong and had poor habits. We know a tree by the fruit that it produces. It is the same with a person. Sports can reveal the content of a person's character. What are you doing to develop a character that will help you (and your team) be successful?

DAK PRESCOTT'S CUP

On November 20, 2016, Dak Prescott, the starting quarterback of the Dallas Cowboys, threw for 300 yards and 3 touchdowns against the Baltimore Ravens. One of his highlights went viral that day. However, it wasn't for anything that he did on-the-field. The CBS cameras caught him doing something that every athlete in America does on a regular basis – he tried to throw a paper cup into a trash bucket about six feet away. Just like nearly every athlete in American, he missed. But unlike nearly every athlete in America, he got up and went over to the trash can and picked the paper cup up off the ground and put it in the trash can.

In that moment, he wasn't thinking that millions of people were watching him. He wasn't doing it for show. He did the right thing. Dak Prescott made a mess, so he cleaned it up. Yes, there are equipment managers and custodians that can clean things up but that doesn't mean we have to add to their work load. That little gesture went a long way toward demonstrating what kind of character Dak Prescott has.

Think about your bench area, dugout, sidelines or locker rooms. There are probably cups and athletic tapes littered all over the place. If your team doesn't care enough about that, then will they really care enough about doing the little things it takes to win games. Taking pride in the little things is how big things are accomplished. It has often been said that how you do anything is how you do everything. It is always the right time to do the right thing.

MICHAEL JORDAN

When Michael Jordan came to the NBA, he was known as just a great athlete and scorer. Defenses were backing off of him and daring him to shoot jumpers. During his first five years in the league, he only made 58 total three-pointers, while shooting a terrible 20.2%. His Chicago Bulls were falling short in the playoffs and not winning as much as their talent suggested. Jordan decided to do something about it and work on his weakness.

In his sixth year, he shot 37.6% and made a total of 92 three-pointers in that season, which was way more than in his previous five seasons combined. He also led the Bulls to the conference championship game during that sixth year and then the NBA Championship the next year. Many players have been prolific scorers and dunkers but few have been deadly from any area on the court. He listened to his coaches and eventually because arguably the greatest player in NBA history.

JULIO JONES HUSTLE

Do you do what's right no matter the situation? If you are a wide receiver, do you come off the line the same whether you are running a pass pattern or blocking for a running back? If you are a baseball hitter, do you run out ground balls to second base as hard as you do when you hit a long grounder to the third baseman? Little daily positive habits lead to long-term success.

The best players do not turn their hustle, talent or work ethic on or off like a light switch. Atlanta Falcons star wide receiver, Julio Jones, is an example of a player that goes hard regardless of the situation or the role that he is asked to play. His offensive coordinator Kyle Shanahan believed that Jones' intangibles are what made him stand apart from others,

> "He's fearless. He doesn't mind the physicality of the game. I think he's one of the best blocking receivers around. You've seen him on picks (against the Falcons), looking like a cyborg going down the field making tackles."

In 2015 against Tampa Bay, Kwon Alexander intercepted a pass 5 yards deep in the end zone and took off the other way. Jones sprinted after him and finally chasing down the linebacker at Atlanta's 12-yard line, running more than 90 yards to make the tackle. The play was nullified by an offside penalty on the Buccaneers, but Atlanta Falcons safety Ricardo Allen noticed something about Julio Jones on that play,

> "He clearly saw the flag was thrown. But the thing he was putting out: You're not going to take the ball from us and go score. You're not going to do that. He didn't have to do that. He could've saved his energy. He could've sat back and watched. But that's just the type of person he is. When he comes to practice, he's running full speed like it's the fourth quarter of the championship game."

COACH DOESN'T GIVE ME CHANCE

Noted philosopher and scholar, Captain Jack Sparrow from the Pirates of the Caribbean, made a statement that is very applicable to sports. He said, "The problem is not the problem. The problem is our attitude toward the problem."

A lot of players are going to get frustrated with their playing time. They are going to disagree with a coach. They are going to struggle in their relationships with teammates. Those are problems that will exist. However, the problem is our attitude toward those adversities. In the story below, both Becky and Sadaria had problems. One choose to maintain a positive attitude about the problem and the other choose to feel sorry for herself,

As a coach, I didn't play a lot of players. My starters received the bulk of the minutes. This had a tendency to cause some frustration for the reserves. However, it also showed me which players were team players and which players were more concerned about themselves. It also showed me which players would continue to work on their games and which would play the victim card, letting the situation dictate their behavior.

In two separate years, I had backup shooting guards (we'll call them Becky and Sadaria). The one year, Becky was playing behind an All-American receiving very little playing time. She thought that she should be playing more and continued to work on her game. She wanted to be ready when her time came, which would eventually happen. The starter was hurt and couldn't play against a nationally-ranked team. Becky stepped in and scored a career-high 28 points on 7 three-pointers. She was ready for her opportunity.

In another year, a similar situation emerged and Sadaria then got her chance to show me what she was capable of. She scored zero points in 28 minutes of playing time. She didn't add much of value in any other areas either. This was not surprising because once she realized that she wasn't going to play much, she stopped working on her game. Every day after practice she would be one of the first to leave. She wasn't prepared for her opportunity and then proved me right as a coach.

RAY ALLEN

On June 19, 2013, it appeared that the San Antonio Spurs were going to win another NBA Championship. They were up 3-2 in the series and were leading the Miami Heat 94-89 with only 0:28 remaining in Game 6. NBA league officials had already brought the Championship trophy to the court for the awards ceremony. Miami clawed its way back in the last half-minute and Ray Allen eventually hit his only three-pointer of the game to force overtime. The Heat would go on to win the game and then win Game 7 to claim the Championship. Game 6 was so epic that the game would eventually receive ESPN's 2013 ESPY award for Best Game.

Even though Ray Allen was toward the end of his career when he joined the Miami Heat and didn't start a single game during that 2012-2013 Championship series. He stayed ready for his opportunity to help his team. He was famous for being the first player to arrive at the gym and the last to leave. His shooting workouts were legendary. It was said that he worked just as hard at the end of his career as he did at the peak of his career. In retrospect, would Miami have won the Championship if Ray Allen hadn't prepared for every game?

Abraham Lincoln has a number of famous quotes about preparation including,

"I will prepare and someday my chance may come."

"If I had 6 hours to cut down a tree, I'd spend the first 4 hours sharpening my blade."

It would seem that Ray Allen took these Abe Lincoln quotes to heart. In an article by Zach Buckley, he presents a story in which Heat coach Erik Spoelstra recalls Allen's preparation,

"He would lay on the floor, pop up, backpedal, have the presence of mind to have his feet set and not out of bounds and have a coach throw him the ball. Afterwards, I said, 'That seemed like a crazy drill.' Why would he do something like that—lay down in the middle of the floor?

He said, 'It's extreme, but I want to prepare myself for when I'm in the lane, I hit the floor, I'm on the ground, offensive rebound that I have the fundamentals to be able to backpedal stay in bounds and be able to knock down shots.'

"It was an incredible thing to see, but that's how Ray Allen was with his workouts. It was on all levels—his conditioning, his shooting, tying it all together, his footwork."

If you watch the clip of the last play in regulation of Game 6, you will see Ray Allen get knocked off balance in the lane on a rebound attempt and then back pedal out to the corner to hit the game-tying three-pointer. His preparation ended up paying off. In fact, it was very similar to the exact drill he regularly practiced.

Ray Allen was a future Hall of Famer that was coming off the bench. He was relegated to being a role player but he played the role perfectly because the goal of winning a championship was much more important than the role that he wanted to play.

KWAHI LEONARD

During the 2015-2016, Kwahi Leonard shot 44.3% from the three-point arc. Only J.J. Redick and Steph Curry shot better. Considering that Leonard was First-Team All-NBA, that hardly seemed strange. However, ~~only~~ a few years earlier he had been a very poor shooter. In his two years at San Diego State University, he shot 20.5% and 29.1% from the three-point arc.

It is a testament to his Leonard's coachability and work ethic that he was willing to honestly evaluate his game and his goals. He wanted to help his team win so much that he was willing to admit his weaknesses and improve on them. When you consider the NBA has better defenders and the line is farther back, Leonard's percentage improvement is even more impressive.

COACH PLAYS FAVORITES

Maybe you've heard someone say "Coach plays favorites". Maybe you've even said it once or twice? The reality is your coach probably does play favorites. Your coach's favorite players are the ones that do what they are supposed to do.

I had a player whom I coached in Tennessee. She was a talented player who loved to shoot three-pointers. However, the strength of our team was our inside game. We were tough to stop inside and we tried to take advantage of this whenever possible. Our rule for three-point shots was that you could only take them if it was called for in a play or if the ball was passed out of the paint. This talented guard that I had did not like my rule. She wanted to "play her game". We had many discussions about this behind closed doors.

It was very clear that she disagreed with me. But you know what? She did what I asked of her and sacrificed for the betterment of the team. Because of this, she became one of my favorite players. She played nearly 40 minutes per game. I rarely took her out because I could rely on her to do what I asked of her even though I knew that she disagreed. She became a favorite of mine because she led herself by doing what was right. Her example also rubbed off on other players.

STEPH CURRY EJECTION

In Game 6 of the 2016 NBA Finals, the league's first-ever unanimous MVP, Steph Curry was ejected. He was frustrated because his team was losing the game, as well as its' grip on the entire series. Curry didn't agree with the officiating and was playing bad.

Overall, he did not handle the situation very well resulting in his night ending early with an ejection. This behavior was not appropriate for a leader as it showed he had lost focus on his goal and instead, started to get distracted by peripheral things. But, it was Curry's comments afterwards that were most concerning.

Good leaders take responsibility for their actions and understand that they, and only they, control their behaviors. His comments reminded me of my pre-marital counseling.

Our pastor said to never follow up an apology with the word "but". It devalues the apology. It minimizes the sentiment and the meaning of saying "I'm sorry". How many times have we said something like the following statement? "Babe, I am sorry that I yelled at you, but if only you _____, then I wouldn't have had to set you straight." As a coach, I saw this often …

"I am sorry that I was late but my roommate didn't set the alarm clock."

"I am sorry that I didn't do well on that test but the teacher didn't remind us about it."

"I am sorry that I was sluggish in the game today but it was just hard to get going early since we started off playing zone."

"I should have been ready when you sent me into the game but I didn't expect to play."

Why do we say "but" after an apology or a statement? It is normally because we are trying to make ourselves look better. We are probably trying to have our cake and eat it too. We want to appear that we are sorry while at the same time making an excuse.

So, coming back to Steph Curry and his comments. For the record, I am a Curry fan. I admire the way he works. I normally like his attitude and often use positive stories about him. So what did Steph Curry say that got me all riled up after he was ejected for throwing his mouthpiece? Here it is,

"I definitely didn't mean to throw it at a fan, but it happened. I went over and apologized to him because that's obviously not where I was trying to take my frustration out. But the last two fouls I had I thought were — I didn't think I fouled either Kyrie [Irving] or LeBron. That's just kind of my perception of the plays and I had a reaction to it."

You might not think this is bad. However, being a leader is all about having a champion's mindset and taking full responsibility for your actions. The official didn't make him throw a mouthpiece. Curry choose to throw the mouthpiece because he had lost focus. We control our actions. Do I think some of the fouls were suspect? Yes, I do. I also know for a fact that he get away from fouls that aren't called, but you don't see him talk about those and thank the officials for not calling them. Players too often focus on the wrong things. We must always be in control of our actions.

Bottom line take away? If we truly want to be more successful, ~~then~~ we must take full responsibility for our actions. When you add a "but" into your statements or make excuses, you don't fully maximize your opportunities.

ANTONIO BROWN FACEBOOK LIVE

On January 15, 2016, after a Pittsburgh Steeler's playoff win to setup an AFC Championship matchup with the New England Patriots, star wide receiver Antonio Brown broadcast coach Mike Tomlin's post-game speech. This speech was like most locker room speeches – obscenity laced, brutally honest, and most importantly, only intended for his team—his family. During the speech, Tomlin had a number of negative things to say about the New England Patriots, while attempting to motivate his guys for the upcoming week. The 17-minute long live video also showed teammates undressing.

Clearly, this was a lapse in judgement by Brown, but it also showed that he was thinking only of himself at that moment and not how his actions could affect the rest of his team. Stunts like this can cause a player to lose the respect of his teammates, thus minimizing his power to positively influence others. It can also serve to give another team like the Patriots, bulletin board material.

Ben Roethlisberger, the Steelers quarterback, summed up the thoughts of many of his teammates when he went on 93.7 the Fan in Pittsburgh and said,

> "It's an unfortunate situation that we've got to deal with right now. That's a sacred place where things are said and hugs and tears, and it's kind of a special place. So a little disappointed with AB for that…Coach talks and then I talk, and you just don't want everyone to know what's going on in there with the family. And also, I wish AB would have been listening to Coach and myself instead of being on the other side of the locker room filming."

Brown wasn't leading himself or doing what was right because he wasn't paying attention to his coach. But he also put the team in jeopardy for the next game by providing bulletin board material for the Patriots and took advantage of his teammate's trust by filming the locker room, a sacred and intimate place for teams. Brown later apologized to the team but the damage had been done and a sacred trust had already been broken.

In his apology, he used a word that is one of the biggest team-killers, "distraction". Brown said that he was "sorry to them for letting it become a distraction and something that they've had to answer questions about while we're preparing for a big game on Sunday." Distractions are what you see when you take your eyes off the goal. Brown's focus turned to himself and he provided a distraction that consumed the Steeler's locker room and practice time for an entire week.

In the AFC Championship, the New England Patriots defeated the Pittsburgh Steelers 36-17 and Brown was held to only 77 yards receiving after averaging 116 yards in the previous two playoff games.

BILLY DONOVAN

Billy Donovan is now known as a successful NBA coach and a former National Championship basketball coach at the University of Florida. However, he first came to the public's eye when he led the underdog Providence Friars to the 1987 NCAA Final Four. He would eventually go on to play in the NBA.

However, his career didn't start off on a good note. Donovan averaged just two points per game as a sophomore. He was out of shape and had a new coach. That new coach, Rick Pitino, told him he had to lose a bunch of weight and get himself in shape if he was going to play in his up-tempo system.

Instead of getting mad and transferring, which he was considering, Donovan decided to stick it out and do what the coach was asking. This paid off as he was a Final Four hero and NBA player. Nobody ever said it would be easy but it is almost always worth it.

PATIENCE REWARDED

Things don't always go the way we would like them to go. When this happens, we have a choice to make. We can quit or make the best of it. Basketball player Frank Kaminsky chose to make the best of it. In Kaminsky's first two seasons, he played only 9 minutes per game averaging 2.9 PPG and 1.5 RPG.

The 7-footer also endured criticism for his lack of production. He didn't transfer. He didn't quit. He didn't bad mouth his coach in the media. He didn't sub-tweet his feelings. No, he just worked harder on his game, stayed focused on his and the team's goals and waited for his opportunity.

Boy, did it pay off as his game blossomed and the right opportunity came his way. During his junior and senior year of college, he led Wisconsin to back-to-back Final Fours. During his senior year, he was college basketball's unanimous Player of the Year and selected 9th in the NBA draft.

Kaminsky is a great example of persevering through adversity and choosing to make the best of difficult situations. He kept preparing so that he could be ready for when his opportunity came. It also reminds me of Luke Maye's story when he became a college basketball legend.

During the 2017 NCAA Men's Basketball Tournament, Kentucky and North Carolina went back and forth for 40 minutes in an Elite Eight game. When Kentucky's freshman sensation Malik Monk hit a crazy, contested, off-balance three-pointer with 7.2 seconds remaining to tie the game, it looked like the fans would be treated to bonus basketball in this instant classic.

However, a former UNC walk-on had something else in mind. Luke Maye, who was averaging only 5.5 PPG while playing only 14 minutes per game, hit a buzzer beating jump shot to win the game for the TarHeels and send them to the Championship game, which they would eventually win. Luke Maye was the eighth-leading scorer for UNC. He was not quite the guy you would expect to be on the court in a crucial situation, let alone become an instant legend for a traditional powerhouse.

Shortly after UNC's last-second loss to Villanova in the 2016 NCAA Championship game, Maye visited coach Roy Williams and vowed to work harder than any player in the program during the offseason. Maye averaged just 1.2 points as a freshman. After his legendary shot, Maye commented about his improvement,

> "Coach always preaches sweat and putting in the time. I put a lot of hours in the gym doing extra shooting, whatever it takes. I always wanted to be ready for a moment like this."

There is no guarantee that if you prepare then your chance will come, however, you can be certain that if you don't prepare then you will not be ready when your opportunity happens to come.

THREE BRICKLAYERS

In his book, *Winning Every Day*, former Notre Dame football coach Lou Holtz told a story about three bricklayers who were asked what they were doing. It is a good illustration of the integrity principle we talked about in chapter 2 and the importance of leading ourselves well,

> The first responded, "I am laying bricks." The second said, "I am making $17.50 an hour." The third said I'm building the most beautiful cathedral in town. Years from now people will be able to come here and worship." Which individual do you think understood his sense of purpose? Which one do you think brought more to his job?

Are you just playing your sport for fun? Are you just doing what coach tells you to do because you are obedient or are you seeing the bigger picture and seeking excellence for yourself and your teammates? There is a related story about an elderly carpenter that was due to retire.

The elderly carpenter told his employer of his plans to leave the business and start a life of leisure with his wife and extended family.

He would miss the money, but the time was right and he was ready to hang up his hammer. His boss was disappointed as the carpenter had been a loyal and diligent worker for many years and was sad to see him go.

The boss asked for one last favor, requesting that the carpenter could build one last house before retiring. The tradesman agreed, but it was soon clear that his heart wasn't in it.

He took shortcuts, used inferior materials and put in a half-hearted effort. In the end, the final product was well short of his usual standards, a disappointing way to end his career.

When the job was finished, the employer came to inspect the work. After taking a look around, he handed the keys to the carpenter and said, "This is your house, it's my gift to you."

The carpenter was shocked and embarrassed. If only he had known, he would have made sure that everything was perfect. If he had known the consequences, he would have demanded excellence from himself.

We are all building something with our lives day by day. Every day we build a wall, lay a brick, construct a house, hammer a nail but are we putting our all into it? Life is oftentimes a DIY project. What you do today makes you who you are tomorrow.

Your attitude can determine the success of a project. Taking pride in a task and having enthusiasm will show in your work. You can't always control the project you're assigned, the drill that you have to do, or the play that coach calls, but you can always control your attitude and your own actions. You can always lead yourself.

TWO PLAYERS MISSING PRACTICE

I once had two different players miss the first practice after Christmas break. They were unrelated and had different reasons for missing. They both came to see me within an hour after practice ended. As I talked with each of the players as they arrived, I found that they had two entirely different approaches and demeanors toward missing practice.

Hannah told me that she was very mad at her parents because they were supposed to wake her up but didn't. Even when I pointed out that she was 21 years old and an adult, she continued to blame her parents. She never once genuinely apologized for missing practice, nor took responsibility for her actions.

Sade was very apologetic. She said that she had no excuse and that she had just failed to wake up on time and that it would never happen again. Two different players. Two different approaches. One took responsibility for her actions. One blamed others.

PERSEVERANCE AND FRUSTRATION

Sometimes you will be frustrated with your season. You might even have a sense of despair or feel there is little hope. Whether these feelings are related to your team or they are because of your own role or performance, you should remember the Jacob Riis' and his quote concerning rock sculptures,

> "Look at a stone cutter hammering away at his rock, perhaps a hundred times without as much as a crack showing in it. Yet at the hundred-and-first blow, it will split in two, and I know it was not the last blow that did it, but all that had gone before".

Just like the stone cutter, you don't always know when good will come but you do know that if you quit, it will never come. Abe Lincoln lost 2 sons and countless political races but persevered through disappointment to become arguably the greatest president in U.S. History. Moses stuttered but overcame that obstacle to become one of the greatest Biblical leaders. Michael Jordan got cut from the team during his sophomore year of high school, yet became a Hall of Fame basketball player.

These are just a few examples of individuals failing forward – of people refusing to quit. What about you? Are you going to keep persevering or are you Darby? You see, R.U. Darby went to California in search of gold and untold riches during the 1800's gold rush.

Every day he got up early in the morning and walked to the hills in search of his "fortune". He dug and dug with his simple tools. He found some gold here and there. But never anything to write home about.

Darby ended up giving up because he was convinced that he would never find the true mother-load that he was searching for. He ended up selling all his tools to another prospector. Picking up where Darby left off, the new prospector discovered that R.U. Darby had been three feet from where the real gold deposit was.

Darby had such high hopes and had sacrificed so much but had quit too early. He was literally three feet away from his dreams. He was so close to the gold, he could reach out and touch it. But there was no way he could know this because he gave up too soon.

Are you Darby or do you have a champion's mindset? You face choices every moment of every day. Will you win the play? Will you win the day? You can choose your actions. You can create your own luck. You can create what happens to you, based on your decisions. You create your future, both by your actions and non-actions. You control you. You have an influence on your friends. You choose to do things the right way. Are you losing the game badly? Are you in the midst of a losing streak? You can still play every play like it is the most important play in the Super Bowl.

One spring day when I was an athletic director, I was watching a baseball game in which we were losing big. Our baseball team was doing better than they had done in many years but still had a losing season. In this particular game, Eli Foreman, our best pitcher, was struggling. Late in the game, he ended up coming to the plate for his turn to hit. He hit a routine ground ball to the short stop. He was definitely going to be out but he busted his tail down to first base. He was out by a mile but I vividly remember him having the personal integrity to play every play like it mattered. He was having a rough day on the mound and the team was losing. However, I will always remember that Eli gave his all when it would have been easy to just coast and go-through the motions or felt sorry for himself.

Feeling sorry for one's self is not the way to handle frustrations or disappointing seasons. It reminded me of a story that I heard in church concerning Karl Menninger. Menninger was a world class psychologist who was on the cover of Time Magazine at one point. He was speaking to a large college class once and afterwards, someone asked him what they should do if they were depressed or distraught. Instead of mentioning counseling, he said to "board up the house, go across the street, find someone in need and go help them."

The only way to beat despair or frustrations is through engagement. Get out of your own little world. Stop being selfish. Help others. Don't point fingers. Add value to others. Do you feel like the coach doesn't praise you enough, then praise others. Find ways to help and lift up others. Leadership begins with you. I encourage you to make a beautiful stone sculpture today by continuing to chip away and pound the rock.

5.

LEADING OTHERS

"The final piece in a championship team is leadership. The most attractive type of leadership to me is the student-athlete who is a coach on the field. I want a driving force who won't let standards slip. That's how teams with ordinary talent can win championships. Without leadership, even a team with great talent will struggle to become a champion."
– Anson Dorrance

"A good leader gets people to follow him because they want to, not because he makes them."
– Tony Dungy

"The best way to find yourself is to lose yourself in the service of others."
– Mahatma Gandhi

"You won't win consistently without good team leadership. It's just that plain and simple. You've got to have players who are willing to buy into your system, demand the best from themselves and their teammates, and hold their teammates accountable."
– Pat Summitt

"Only a life lived for others is worth living."
– Albert Einstein

It is not just enough to lead yourself effectively, you must also have a positive influence on others. John C. Maxwell says "A leader without followers is just someone taking a nice walk." If you are a captain or an upperclassman, this will be obvious. However, if you are a player that doesn't have any kind of positional leadership, then this might seem difficult to do. You understand that you have to lead yourself and you are committed to doing what is right. But, lead others? How are you supposed to do that?

Every player has close friends on their team. You might not be good friends with every one of your teammates but you do have some close friendships. Those are going to be the people that you lead most effectively. We are influenced by people that we like and trust. You might not be able to influence every member of your team but you will be able to lead some of them. Those of the ones that you need to focus the majority of your attention on. Your positive (or negative) influence will be most evident among your circle of friends.

The first step to being a leader is to lead yourself. The next step is to lead others. In particular, those that you are closest to. If you are leading yourself the wrong way, then you will lead your friends the wrong way. You will either be the ringleader of bad choices or you will allow poor choices to be made while you remain quiet and approving of the actions.

Ultimately, you will become like the people that you hang out with the most and they will become like you. The ideal situation is that you and your friends are influencing each other in a positive way. If this is not the case, then the question becomes, who will have the most influence? Even in situations where a group of friends are not all positive influences, there is still some type of influence going on. Either you are influencing your friends positively or they are influencing you in a less than positive manner. You must lead others positively in order to have a chance to create that championship culture on your team that you desire. Granted, you can't do it by yourself.

You also can't lead everyone because you won't have a friendship or strong connection with everyone on the team. Those you have the strongest connection with are the ones that you will be able to lead most effectively. You might say, "the team won't listen to me" and you might be right. However, your friends will listen to you. The wonderful thing about that is you just might be starting a chain reaction that ends up with the whole team listening to you without them even knowing that. It is rare that a group of friends is completely self-contained and doesn't have strong relationships with others. For example, your three closest friends all probably have at least one other person that they are close to that you aren't as close with. This ripple effect is how your influence can eventually influence an entire team.

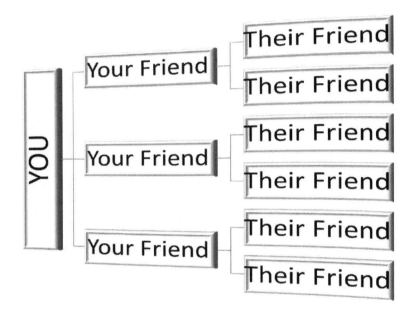

LARRY FITZGERALD

The wide receiver position in football typically requires a look-at-me attitude and a whole lot of bravado. A lot of people sure looked at the Arizona Cardinals' Larry Fitzgerald but it was not because he sought out the limelight or exhibited brash behavior. Larry Fitzgerald certainly had an aura of look-at-me but it wasn't in the way you would generally think.

He didn't demand the ball, respect or attention by holding press conferences, sub-tweeting his feelings or yelling at people on the sidelines. He let his actions speak louder than his words. He got passes because it helped the team, not because he demanded to be thrown to. His work ethic and positive attitude were well-known.

Josh Weinfuss of ESPN.com wrote a really good article outlining Fitzgerald's work ethic and example. Not only does Fitzgerald lead himself but it rubs off on his teammates according to his coach Bruce Arians,

"You see guys creating foundations and doing things in the community to try to model his, which is tough to model. But more than anything, all our wide receivers block. Everybody practices hard, especially in that room, and that's what you ask of all your veterans, is to set an example in your room. He's as good as it gets."

His teammates have definitely noticed. During J.J. Nelson's rookie year as a wide receiver for the Arizona Cardinals, he took note of Fitzgerald's work ethic and it helped shape his outlook on playing in the NFL.

"He's 30-plus and he comes in each and every day to work," Nelson said. "To me, that made me feel like I don't have any excuses. I feel like I should do the same thing."

Arizona Cardinals center A.Q. Shipley echoes much of J.J. Nelson's sentiments concerning Larry Fitzgerald's example,

"Just watching him practice, watching him come to work every day, watching him in the training room, he's the consummate pro. It's incredible watching a guy who's played as long as he has in the league going out on a Thursday when we're not in pads, diving for balls, never taking a play off in practice.

Are you a player that others look at and see behavior that they want to model? Larry Fitzgerald had a positive influence on his teammates because of his work ethic and attitude. He doesn't even have to say a word for teammates to follow him.

JERRY RICE

Jerry Rice is considered the greatest wide receiver in the history of the NFL. In fact, many people would argue that he is the greatest football players ever, period. His work ethic was well-known, which partially enabled him to play at a high level for 20 years even though he wasn't considered the fastest or the strongest. One of his former coaches, Mike Shanahan, described his work ethic,

> "Every day during the off-season, Jerry would be up a 6:00 AM going through his strenuous stretching drills. He would run seven 5-yard shuttles, which he called "stop and go's," and fourteen more 40-yard dashes up and down the field. Then he would line up fluorescent orange cones across the field and weave in and out of each one six times at full speed, working on his acceleration and cutting ability. When he finished with the cones, he would run six more 40-yard dashes, and then 20-yard patterns until he was flat-out exhausted.

> Then he would lift weights in as quick a rotation as possible, no resting. Bench presses, seated bench presses, incline bench press, power lifts, dumbbell curls with increasing weights. I get tired just writing about it. It didn't take me long to understand why every time we got to the fourth quarter of a game, while most of the players were slowing down, Jerry could run as fast he did on the first play of the game."

Jerry Rice didn't have the 40-yard dash time and some wondered if he wasn't faster with pads on than when he was just on a track. In all seriousness, though, having a work ethic like Rice did explains a lot of his success. Certainly, he had talent but relative to some of the other receivers in the league, he didn't have as much. His work ethic allowed him to be faster and stronger when it mattered. He worked religiously for years so that he could play at a high level for years.

JULIO JONES

In week 4 of the 2016 NFL season, Atlanta Falcons wide receiver Julio Jones became just the 6th player in NFL history to amass 300 yards receiving in a single-game. He would go on to lead the Falcons to the Super Bowl and earn his 4th Pro Bowl appearance in only his sixth season. One of his role models growing up was Jerry Rice. Just like Rice, Julio Jones is known for his unassuming nature, his toughness in playing through injuries and his incredible work ethic. In an ESPN.com interview, Jones had this to say about his game and that of Rice's,

> "You've got to go out there and play the game the way it's supposed to be played. Then you get people to like you and appreciate your work by just going out there and competing every down. Jerry Rice was looked at in that perspective. He went out there and was a hard-working guy. He was going to give it his all. And I'm kind of the same way. I just go out and give my all, no matter what happens. So many people are going to always remember what you do and how you make them feel instead of you telling them this and telling them that. That's why I like to go out and show the work ethic and how I am as a teammate. That's how you become great."

Julio Jones cares about winning more than stats. This rubs off on his teammates. During the 2016 season, 13 different Atlanta Falcons caught touchdown passes, which was an NFL record. The Falcons were able to have a great season because they were a true team and this couldn't be accomplished if the star player wanted the limelight to himself. Head coach Dan Quinn saw this trait in Jones early on when he first took over the Falcons,

> "The thing that people on the outside don't know is what kind of teammate he is and why he's held in such high regard inside this building. It's because of the way he works. He's got this unbelievable work ethic that carries over into everything he does. In meetings, he's locked in. On the field, he's locked in. I think it's a pretty rare guy that has the ability to stay locked in for long periods of time."

HAZING

The National Federation of High School Associations defines hazing as any "humiliating or dangerous activity expected of a student to belong to a group, regardless of their willingness to participate". Though there have been way too many deaths as a result of "innocent" hazing activities, physical harm is not the only barometer of whether hazing occurred. Emotional or mental issues resulting from hazing can last for years. Hazing can lead to mistrust, fear, lack of self-confidence, stress, and anxiety. Those are not qualities that you want your teammates to be experiencing if you want to win a championship ring at the end of the year.

Some of the typical hazing activities are head-shaving, piercing, "kidnapping", deprivation of or consummation of food and drink, tattooing, inappropriate physical touching or behavior, as well as other embarrassing acts. Unfortunately, these hazing activities are justified by saying that "boys will be boys" or "it's just kids being kids" or "it helps with team bonding and brings us together." Remember that the definition of hazing includes a humiliating activity.

More than 1.5 million high school students admit that they have experienced some form of hazing in their lifetime. However, the real number is probably much higher because many kids do not admit to being hazed or buy into the lie that it is just team bonding. Successful teams are built and teammates bond when they are aligned toward positive common goals. When activities encourage others, promote the team over the individual, teach positive lessons, build respect for others, promote friendship and create an environment for growth, then you are building a team that can be successful.

Nearly every player will say that they don't want their coaches or parents to be negative or sarcastic toward them. Players don't want to be embarrassed by them. Players don't want to be motivated by fear or punishment. They want to be supported, encouraged, praised and motivated by rewards and hope. Positive motivation is long-term, while motivation because of fear is short-lived. However, those same players that believe in hazing will fall into the same trap and believe that fear, punishment or embarrassment will bond players. This might have a short-term effect but will definitely not work in the best interest of the individuals or the team long-term.

Think about your best friend(s) right now. Most of the time, you became best friends through positive circumstances. You've bonded over common interests and getting to know each other. The same is true for a team. Playing cards in a hotel room on the road, sharing jokes on a bus ride, encouraging one another when things are tough can serve to bond a team. You have opportunities all around you to take advantage of that are positive. In addition to the normal occurrences that can bond a team, there are thousands of ways that a team can bond that are positive and have a proven track record of success. Just a few of these include:

- Mentorship programs (big brothers/big sisters)
- Community Service
- Special nights of hanging out (without hazing or illegal activities)
- Watch a sporting event together (live or on TV)
- Celebrate successes or special occasions
- Organize a camp for young athletes in the community
- Promote a cause
- Design a t-shirt or motto for the year
- Laser tag
- Team retreats
- Engage in team functions outside of the season
- Adopt-A-Team at your school. (Bake cookies, decorate lockers, write notes, etc…)

Here are some myths about hazing according to the National Federation of High School Associations. If you think hazing has anything to do with bonding or friendship, you're caught up in the myths about hazing. At its best, hazing builds resentment between new members and initiates. At its worst, hazing can seriously injure or kill:

Myth: They (newcomers) want to be hazed. **Reality:** No one wants to be abused, humiliated or embarrassed.

Myth: We only haze a little bit. It's really not that bad. **Reality:** That's like saying, "I only steal a little bit. I'm not really a thief."

Myth: If we eliminate hazing, our members will be just like anybody else. **Reality:** A truly well organized, positive program results in initiates who are eager to work for and help the group, and who can better serve as leaders.

Myth: If new members don't respect our principles or us, we haze them until they improve. **Reality:** Hazing a new member makes the situation worse. Just like other forms of victimization, hazing breeds mistrust, apathy, and alienation, not respect.

Myth: Hazing activities are the only methods we have of controlling the new members. **Reality:** There are positive and negative ways to bring people into the fold. "You catch more flies with honey than with vinegar." Accountability should be the same for new members and ongoing members.

Myth: I went through it, so now the new members have to go through it. **Reality:** It only takes one group of "veterans" to break this so-called tradition. The people who founded your group were not hazed. Why treat today's new members differently?

It doesn't matter if you were hazed when you were younger or that it has always been done that way. You might have had to carry the bags as a freshman or were taped to the goal posts in football. You shouldn't have been hazed in the past but nothing can be done about what happened to you now. But you can do something about the present and the future to eliminate the negatives that hazing can bring about.

The old Chinese proverb says that the best time to plant a tree is 20 years ago but that the second best time to plant a tree is now. What will you do to influence yourself and your teammates positively? How will you help create a championship culture on your team? You might not be able to do everything, but you can do something. What good will you do today?

LEN BIAS

Who is the best basketball player that you've ever seen? Most would say Michael Jordan, Lebron James, Magic Johnson or Wilt Chamberlin. If you have seen ESPN's 30-for-30 entitled "Without Bias" then you would know that there are many that consider Len Bias the best college basketball player they ever saw. However, we were all left to ask ourselves "what if" when it came to Bias' professional career. Here is his story as told by Kevin Templeton in the book *To The Hilt,*

Jordan was not the best college player I ever saw. Len Bias of Maryland would hold that distinction. Bias was a better college player because he was a better shooter than Jordan, a more dominant rebounder than Jordan, and bigger and stronger than M.J. Len Bias was like Michael Jordan on steroids. He was six eight and weighed 210 pounds. He was one of the first basketball players to lift weights during the season. (Before this time it was thought by many that lifting weights during the season would throw off your shot.) He could score inside or outside. He was ultracompetitive and an unselfish team player.

He led Maryland to its zenith in basketball honors as the Terps won the ACC Tournament. Bias was an All-American as well as the Atlantic Coast Conference's player of the Year twice. He was the ACC Athlete of the year for all sports in 1986. He had unparalleled athletic ability and size, yet he also had a tremendous knowledge of how to play the game. Bias was as fierce a competitor as you will ever see playing any sport as well.

On June 17, Bias was selected as the second overall pick in the 1986 NBA Draft by the defending NBA champion Boston Celtics. A new shoe company wanted Bias to be the face of their aggressive advertising campaign. They wanted to challenge industry giants Nike and Adidas. The new company was Reebok. Bias agreed to wear Reebok shoes exclusively and film three commercials for Reebok in exchange for $1.6 million over five years. He also would receive tens of thousands of dollars worth of Reebok shoes and gear form himself as well as his friends and family.

Two days after the draft Bias went out to celebrate with some friends and teammates. His dad told him, "Be careful. Be careful what you do; be careful who you are with." Bias returned to his dorm in Washington Hall at three a.m. A long-time workout partner and friend, Brian Tribble, had some cocaine. He knew Bias didn't use drugs, but he figured Bias might be interested in trying it since they were celebrating. He warned Bias that this cocaine was very pure and very powerful. "I'm a horse, Trib. I can take it."

But Bias couldn't take it; he had a seizure and collapsed around 6;25 a.m. At 6:32, when Tribble made the 9-1-1 call to get an ambulance, Bias was unconscious and not breathing. He was put on a ventilator to breathe for him, but all attempts at restarting his heart failed. He was pronounced dead at Leland Memorial Hospital in Riverdale, Maryland, at 8:55 a.m. The official cause of death was cardiac arrhythmia related to his cocaine use. He was twenty-two years of age.

Two former girlfriends and numerous teammates said they had never known of Bias ever to use drugs at any time. He took a lot of pride in maintaining his strength and conditioning. Three different NBA teams had tested him prior to the draft, and there was no trace of drugs in his system. Keith Gatlin, Bias's friend and teammate, stated that he had been to Bias's home, had been with him year-round for three years and had taken him to his home in North Carolina, but had never once see Bias use drugs of any kind. Bias had never used drugs prior to June 18.

His family got no money from the Celtics. He never played a game for them. They got no money from Reebok. He never shot a commercial for them. He gave up his future because of a person he thought was his friend.

Nobody had a bright future than Len Bias. He had unmatched athletic gifts, an amazing work ethic, and the competitive drive of an assassin. His magnetic personality and humble demeanor would attract endorsement jobs from major corporations like moths to a flame.

But Len Bias had a friend. That friend, Brian Tribble, was a drug dealer who later served ten years in prison for drug trafficking.

Four days after Bias's death, more than eleven thousand people attended his memorial service at Cole Field House, where he had starred for the University of Maryland. His death was a shock to the nation. I still remember where I was when I heard Len Bias had died.

Len Bias lost his life at age twenty-two. I would guess at least $250 million in future earnings and endorsements were lost. He is not remembered for all the great things he achieved and all the ability he had been blessed with. He is remembered for the dumbest thing he ever did. He made a bad choice, and it cost him his life. Choose friends who will be lifters who encourage you to greater heights. This is crucial because your future might depend on your friends. We will never know what great things Len could have accomplished had he not had a friend named Brian Tribble.

With Templeton's permission, I included this entire portion of his book *To The Hilt* because there are so many details and thoughts that go into the downfall of a person. Such a sad tale for a player that might have been the best-ever! Bias seemed to have the world in the palm of his hand. But he made a poor choice about who he would hang out with, which then led to another poor choice to be influenced by this so-called friend. Brian Tribble, a drug dealer, would not be considered a leader of the Boston Celtics. However, because of his influence on one player, it changed the course of the Boston Celtics franchise for many years to come.

DARRANT WILLIAMS
Early on the morning of January 1, 2007 after the last game of the season,

some San Francisco 49ers were celebrating at a club. At some point, the celebrating went wrong and an altercation occurred with some gang members. A little while later as the players left the club, they continued the confrontation before getting into a limo to leave. One of the gang members got into an SUV and chased down the limo. He fired his gun into the limo killing Darrent Williams, a 24-year old defensive back and kick returner.

Our coaching staff emphasized having each other's back and helping out a teammate. One year, a player of ours got into a fight in the cafeteria with someone that wasn't on the team. About four other players jumped into the fray. Security was called and the players ended up being suspended by the school. When we talked to them after the altercation, they told us that they were just doing what we had told them to do – have each other's backs. However, they had missed the point. In that situation, a true friend and teammate would help you by getting you out of a potentially dangerous or compromising position. A real teammate would have your back by keeping you from doing something that you would later regret.

In the heat of the moment, the player that was initially involved in the fight may not be thinking straight but her teammates should be. They ended up having to sit out a number of games which negatively affected our chances to win the conference title that year. You can have an influence on your friends that help them. There is no shame in walking away from a situation that will negatively impact your goals and dreams.

By all accounts, Darrent Williams was a well-liked and respected member of the Denver Broncos. In fact, there is the Darrent Williams Memorial Teen Center in Denver that helps the youth. The Broncos even named an award in his honor called the Darrent Williams Good Guy Award. He and his other teammates that fateful night was having fun like so many other players do at night. However, friends have a lot of influence on each other. They can influence each other's choices and decisions. They can also re-inforce the current action by not doing anything. Not doing anything is still a choice. One has to wonder how this (or the situation with our players) could have been prevented. Too often, we get caught up in the moment and forget about the bigger picture. Friends have to look out for one another by keeping each other out of compromising positions.

Unfortunately, there are too many stories of athletes that have had their careers and seasons altered because of poor choices when they had so-called friends around them that might have been able to change the situation if they had used their influence for the better. In some cases, lives were lost because friends co-signed the behavior by actively encouraging it or by not speaking up and exerting their influence on the situation.

DRIVING FAST

We all are probably guilty of doing some crazy things once in a while. These are some things that we do that we really don't give much thought to. Sometimes we do these crazy things with our friends. Most of the time, there are not lasting adverse effects to our poor decisions to do crazy things.

Sometimes though, that water fight indoors turns sour when an athlete slips on the wet floor and gets hurt. Sometimes that innocent prank ends up with a suspension or even a misdemeanor arrest on your record. Other times, having a little fun with friends can lead to much worse than a tarnished reputation.

There is a lot of competition for NBA roster spots, so for anyone to stay in the league for nine years was quite the accomplishment. Bobby Phills was a ferocious defensive player but it also didn't hurt that he averaged 11.0 points throughout his career and shot 39% from the three-point arc. Not only was he a very good NBA basketball player but everyone seemed to have a different story about how giving and caring the 6'5", 220 pound Charlotte Hornet was.

After practice on January 12, 2000, Phills and long-time friend and teammate, David Wesley raced off in their Porsches. At speeds approaching 100 mph, just less than one-mile from the Charlotte Coliseum, in a 45-mph speed zone, Phills lost control and hit another vehicle head-on. He died instantly. Witnesses said that the two friends were racing each other. Wesley was ultimately convicted of reckless driving. Lives were changed. Three children lost a father. A team lost one of its' stars. A friend had to live with those memories and regrets.

It is okay to have fun with friends, but we must always stay grounded and think about what we are doing. We tend to do dangerous or crazy stuff when we are around other friends. This doesn't happen as much when we are alone. How much are we influencing our friends? How much are our friends influencing us? Are we influencing in a safe and positive way?

JOE MONTANA

Good leaders absolutely must provide a good example to those around them. If they are not modeling the appropriate behaviors, then they will never be able to gain the respect of their peers. Not every leader will be a rah-rah leader. Joe Montana was one of the greatest quarterbacks of all-time as he won four Super Bowls with the San Francisco 49ers. He was able to orchestrate 31 fourth-quarter comebacks in his career. Part of being such a successful quarterback was his ability to lead his teammates.

For a guy that was fairly quiet, this would seem difficult to do in a sport like football. However, Montana was able to influence because the guys respected him. In his book, *The Score Takes Care of Itself*, Bill Walsh said this about his star quarterback,

> Joe Montana is one of the best examples I have ever seen that proved you don't need to shout, stomp, or strut to be a great leader - just do the job and treat people right.

Joe Montana knew what kind of leadership his team needed. If they needed someone to step up and say something then he would do it. Regardless, though, he was always leading by example. If you are not leading by example then you will never be able to positively lead through your words.

6.
LEADING
REGARDLESS OF
YOUR ROLE

"Not every player can be a star player, but every player must be a star at their role."
— Jay Bilas

"I tell our guys every day: Every person on the roster can help us win a game by making just one play."
— Steve Kerr

""A life isn't significant except for its impact on other lives."
— Jackie Robinson

"Everybody can be great because anyone can serve."
— Martin Luther King, Jr.

"You have a choice to make when you're not playing. Either you're invested and a great teammate or you're not."
— Brad Stevens

"The assumption that change has to start at the top is wrong. Start where you are."
— Jessi Lynn Stoner

L eadership is merely influence, nothing more nothing less. Anyone can have influence. Your team is going to have a coach. Your team is going to have captains. Your team is going to have upperclassmen. Your team is probably going to have stars. However, the majority of players on a team do not have traditional leadership status.

Even though the army has ranks and positions, they still teach the concept that everyone is a leader, no matter how far down the totem pole that they function. The lowliest privates are leaders. If they do their job and do it well, they have a positive influence on those around them—they're leaders

Role players win and lose more games than the "stars". The stars often cancel each other out. The team whose role players help on defense, hit the glass relentlessly, set the tough screens, get the loose balls, stick to their man, and hustle back in transition is usually the team that wins a basketball game.

It is the same with a team that has leaders willing to do the little things. A team with captains willing to do the little things will probably have a championship culture resulting in winning seasons. However, the majority of players on the team are not captains. These players will perform leadership roles that help the team win. The more that they embrace these roles, then the more they increase their opportunities for success.

EVERYONE CAN DO THESE THINGS

Early in my career as a coach, I met with some respected coaches and some of my players and we came up with a list of characteristics that make up a good captain. Once we finalized this one sheet of expectations, my staff realized that it really wasn't specific to captains. Nearly everything that we were asking of our captains, we were also expecting out of our other players. Additionally, there wasn't really anything on the list that a non-captain couldn't own for themselves. This is the not the complete list, but regardless of your role, you can do the following things on your team…

- Committed to teammates and program.
- Represent the program, team, and university on and off the court.
- Enthusiastic and passionate about our basketball program.
- Do not have to be vocal but must be willing to verbalize something when necessary.

- Communicate respectfully and effectively.
- Must value the team's success as much as their own.
- Build and maintain the confidence of their teammates.
- Constructively confront teammates when necessary.
- Maintain poise and composure during stress and adversity.
- Willing to consistently do the right thing.

THE 5 LEVELS OF LEADERSHIP

In John C. Maxwell's 100 books, he has provided leadership insights and principles that have shaped millions. Perhaps none have been as impactful than his concept of The 5 Levels of Leadership. It really provided a different perspective on leadership. You don't have to be a captain or a coach to be a leader. Anyone can be a leader. Here are Maxwell's 5 Levels of Leadership with number one being the most basic and least effective,

1. Position (rights) – People follow you because they have to.
2. Permission (relationships) – People follow you because they want to.
3. Production (results) – People follow because of what you have done for the organization.
4. People Development (reproduction) – People follow because of what you have done for them.
5. Pinnacle (respect) – People follow because of who you are and what you represent.

Your goal shouldn't be to get selected as your team's captain. That alone would only put you as a level 1 leader. Your goal is to become a level-5 leader that has influence because you are so well-respected and have the character of someone that people can believe in. Certainly, you can be a level-5 leader as a captain, but a position or title is not necessary for having true influence on your team.

RUNNING SPRINTS FOR TURNOVERS

One of the teams that I coached decided that they would run sprints for every turnover that they committed in the previous game. They did this for the first game. However, after having a number of turnovers in the second game, the captains decided they didn't want to run any more. I asked a freshman after the game why she didn't run even though she had committed to doing so. Her response was as you would expect...no one else was doing it so why should she?

She went on say that she was only a freshman and had no pull with the other girls. I then pointed out that her two best-friends were on the team and that surely they would have run with her. One of those girls also is close with another team member, who might be good friends with another team member and so on. The law of influence multiplied out might have affected the majority of the team. Doing what is right has to start somewhere. Why not be the one to start it.

HARRIET TUBMAN

Anyone can lead regardless of their role because everyone has the ability to influence. If people respect you and believe in you, then your opportunities to influence increase exponentially. Consider the case of Harriet Tubman. She was a very small, black woman living in the middle 1800's. It is nearly impossible to be further from a traditional leadership position than she was.

Yet, she is one of the greatest leaders of all-time because she was so greatly respected and elicited hope in her followers. Because of her ability to influence others, she saved many lives. She was barely five feet tall yet she commanded the attention of everyone that she came into contact. She wasn't educated but was smart, savvy and wise. She didn't have an official title but became the most well-known conductor of the Underground Railroad. She took great pride in the work that she did to free slaves.

> "I was the conductor of the Underground Railroad for eight years, and I can say what most conductors can't say; I never ran my train off the track and I never lost a passenger."

She inspired or helped hundreds of southern slaves find their freedom in the North during the Civil War. Tubman was affectionately called "Moses" because she went into the land of captivity and broke the chains of slavery for so many people. In 2016, the U.S. Department of Treasury announced that she would replace former President Andrew Jackson on the $20 bill.

How does a someone with a small physical stature and no position of authority end up leaving such a legacy? Tubman found a cause and sacrificed everything to make the world a better place for the people that she could impact. She couldn't save everyone but she could do her part.

MONMOUTH BENCH

You are a talented player but you are not starting. What do you do? When you are part of a team, you are faced with the choice each and every day as to whether you will put yourself first or the team first. This is very obvious when you are "riding the pine". Watch a player's body language and you can see where their thoughts are and what is occupying their focus. The reserves on any team are a big part of the success or failure of that team. The bench can energize and inspire those that are out there playing. The bench players can also bring a team down. As a bench player, you are either an energy-giver or an energy-taker.

One great example of a bunch of guys turning their situation into a positive is when the 2015 version of the Monmouth University men's basketball team. Monmouth might not be Duke or Kentucky, but they are still a NCAA Division I filled with talented players who have worked hard, are proud and want to play. In November of 2015, Monmouth pulled off a huge upset when they defeated Notre Dame. This helped them earn the program's first-ever Top-25 ranking. Head Coach King Rice, who was a starting point guard for the North Carolina Tarheels, had this to say in an ESPN interview,

> "I tell everybody on our team that everybody's role is as important as everyone else's, whether you're the last guy or the first guy. That's their role, to get us going on the bench and having the bench involved in the game. This is a new age, how kids are and they're having a blast. I truly think it helps our team."

Deon Jones, one of the best players in the Metro Atlantic Athletic Conference who eventually played professionally overseas, said this in a Washington Post interview,

> "It is bringing us even more together. We're always talking about it after the game. It shows how everybody is on board

for the team, whether you're playing or on the bench. Because those guys are doing it for us. They didn't do that just to get media attention. They were doing it just to pump us up. And it happened to blow up like this, which is awesome."

On a special aired on the CBS evening news, Steve Noack, who appeared in 27 games as a freshman but would sit out the entire 2015-16 season with an injury said that the bench energy helped the players on the court,

> "Absolutely, it's fun for everyone that is involved. So they are on the other side of it, they are playing and they're grinding. But if they look over at the bench and see that we're in the game, we are energized and try and feed energy to them. They are going to be like 'Wow, if they are in it how can I not be in it?'"

THE MAN WHO THINKS HE CAN

Too many athletes look at their situation and don't step up to be a leader because they are not the star. They are not the captain. Maybe they have self-confidence issues or feel that it isn't their place because they are only a freshman, only a reserve or a newcomer on the team. These are just excuses that distract us from doing what is right and using who we are to influence others in a positive way.

Zig Zigler, the great salesman and motivational speaker used to talk about having a positive mindset and that whether you thought you could do something or thought you couldn't do something, then you probably were right. He might have been inspired in his way of thinking from a poem by Walter D. Wintle,

> If you think you are beaten, you are
> If you think you dare not, you don't,
> If you like to win, but you think you can't
> It is almost certain you won't.
> If you think you'll lose, you're lost
> For out of the world we find,
> Success begins with a fellow's will

It's all in the state of mind.
If you think you are outclassed, you are
You've got to think high to rise,
You've got to be sure of yourself before
You can ever win a prize.
Life's battles don't always go
To the stronger or faster man,
But soon or late the man who wins
Is the man WHO THINKS HE CAN!

A SIMPLE GESTURE

You don't have to be a coach, a star player or a captain to have a positive influence on someone. Here is a story that I read in Jim Tressel's *The Winner's Manual*. It was originally written by John W. Schlatter,

> Mark was walking home from school one day when he noticed the boy ahead of him had tripped and dropped all of the books he was carrying along with two sweaters, a baseball bat, a glove, and a small tape recorder. Mark knelt down and helped the boy pick up the scattered articles. Since they were going the same way, he helped to carry the burden.

> As they walked Mark discovered the boy's name was Bill, that he loved video games, baseball, and history, that he was having a lot of trouble with his other subjects and that he had just broken up with his girlfriend. They arrived at Bill's home first and Mark was invited in for a Coke and to watch some t.v. The afternoon passed pleasantly with a few laughs and some shared small talk, then Mark went home.

> They continued to see each other around school, had lunch together once or twice. They ended up at the same High school where they had brief contacts over the years. Finally, the long awaited senior year came, and three weeks before graduation, Bill asked Mark if they could talk. Bill reminded him of the day years ago when they had first met.

"Do you ever wonder why I was carrying so many things from school that day?" asked Bill. "You see, I cleaned out my locker because I didn't want to leave a mess for anyone else. I had stored away some of my mother's pills and I was going home to commit suicide. But after we spent some time together I realized that if I had, I would have missed that time and so many others that might follow. So you see, Mark, when you picked up my books for me that day, you did a lot more. You saved my life."

Just a little bit of kindness and concern for people saved a life. Mark had no role in this kid's life. Mark wasn't a star football player or student council president. He wasn't out to save the world. Mark was just a boy that wanted to do the right thing. That right thing led to a friendship. What he didn't know at the time was that doing the right thing would influence another person to continue living life.

We might not encounter as serious of a situation during our life, but how about the teammate that is thinking about quitting but hasn't told anyone? Maybe an encouraging word will be just they need to hear. Maybe a player is a selfish teammate but they see your kindness and start to wonder about your attitude and that eventually changes them? You never know how great an effect you can have when you care about people and do the right thing.

EMMITT SMITH HALL OF FAME SPEECH
Statistically speaking, Emmitt Smith is the best running back to ever play in the NFL. In his 15 seasons, he gained 18,355 rushing yards and scored 164 rushing touchdowns. Both of these are records and will most likely never be broken. Smith also won three Super Bowls with the Dallas Cowboys. During his induction speech to the Pro Football Hall of Fame in Canton, Ohio on August 7, 2010, he highlighted what true leadership is all about when he called out his former teammate, Daryl "Moose" Johnston,

> "Daryl Johnston, where are you? Will you please stand? You mean the world to me (tearing up) not just because we shared the same backfield, but because you sacrificed so

much for me. People don't understand what it took to be a fullback in our system, the sacrifices you made not simply with your body but your whole spirit. You took care of me as though you were taking care of your little brother. Without you, without you, I know today would not have been possible. I love you from the bottom of my heart."

Johnston was an All-American running back at Syracuse that would be drafted in the second-round by the Cowboys in 1989. He became the first fullback to ever get selected to the NFL Pro Bowl. He played all ten seasons with the Cowboys. "Moose" played in 149 straight games from the time he was drafted until he got injured in 1997.

In today's NFL, the fullback position has gone the way of the dinosaur. There was a time, however, when many teams utilize the fullback to be the lead blocker for their star tailback. If they were lucky they would get one or two carries per game. Their main purpose was to sacrifice their body and create a better hole for the star to run through. An offensive lineman would often time be matched up nose-to-nose with a defender. However, the fullback would have a 5-10 yard running start and then crash into a defender that was typically bigger. This violent collision was repeated over and over again, especially with Johnston and the Cowboys since no one in NFL history carried the ball more than Emmitt Smith.

It was a tremendous gesture by Smith to praise Johnston during his Hall of Fame speech. He understood that role players are the key to a team's success. Darryl Johnston will probably never be inducted into the Hall of Fame as a player but he definitely was a Hall of Fame teammate. Even though he was not a superstar player for the Cowboys, he played his role to the best of his ability and have a tremendously positive impact on his teammates. Even though he was a role player, he was definitely one of the Dallas Cowboys' Most Valuable Leaders!

I WANT TO WIN MORE THAN ANYTHING

At the end of one of my years of coaching, I was conducting individual meetings with players. As I was meeting with Julie, one of our more mature and respected players, she was telling me how all she wanted to do was win a championship the next year. We had the potential because we had a bunch of talented newcomers returning. Julie said that she was willing to do whatever it took to win because that meant the world to her. She even mentioned that she was willing to sacrifice her playing time or role on the team to make that happen. I was happy to hear that.

As we continued to talk, Julie told me that I needed to do something in the off-season to curb some of the alcohol and drug use that was going on with some of her team members. This was a surprise to me. Once she told me some more details and who they players were, it made more sense to me because they had been very inconsistent toward the end of the year. As more details came out, I became more and more disappointed because there were a number of teammates that knew about this use and had even been at the parties but didn't do anything to stop them. Julie told me that a couple of them had even talked about it but were worried that if they said anything to me that they'd be considered snitches but if they said anything to the girls with the problems, that they might have their friendship questioned. Julie admitted that she also felt this way.

This kind of thing happens often with friends. They are scared to confront or hold their friend accountable because it is either uncomfortable or that they are afraid of losing the friendship. However, if you truly are a friend then you want the best for your friend. Julie wasn't the best player on the team. Julie wasn't a star or even a starter. Julie wasn't even a team captain, but she was a friend. But at the end of the day, she chose her feelings and her comfort level over the welfare of her friends. She was more concerned about herself than she was in trying to help her friends. Sometimes your role on the team is to be a friend that acts like a true friend.

Additionally, from a pure basketball stand point, Julie had said that her number one priority was to win a championship. If that was truly the case then I would be very upset at my "friends" for sabotaging that goal through their poor choices and bad behavior. Winning a championship wasn't as important to Julie as her desire to hang out and have fun with her teammates – who were costing her a chance at a championship.

CHAMPIONSHIP INFLUENCED BY WALK-ON

When John Calipari left the University of Memphis to coach men's basketball at the University of Kentucky, his replacement was Josh Pastner. Pastner would eventually move to the ACC to lead Georgia Tech. Pastner has had success as a big-time NCAA Division I basketball coach but he didn't always have glamorous leadership position. Yes, he has a NCAA championship ring from his playing days at the University of Arizona but he wasn't the one scoring the baskets or dishing out the assists. However, as a player, Pastner may have been just as valuable as some of his more famous teammates, including Jason Terry, Mike Bibby, Michael Dickerson and Miles Simon.

Pastner was a walk-on who averaged 0.9 points per game in his four-year career for the Wildcats, but what he did as a freshman would prove to be valuable. He had a key to the McKale Center so he would get the stars together and they would shoot nightly at the arena. This was key to a season that would eventually see the Wildcats knock off three #1 seeds in North Carolina, Kentucky, and Kansas on their way to winning the 1997 National Championship. This was even more remarkable when you consider that Arizona only finished 5th in their conference that year and entered the NCAA Tournament as a 4th seed. Here is how Doug Haller of the *Arizona Republic* would describe it,

> Freshmen Josh Pastner and Mike Bibby began shooting at night. Just the two of them. At the university's McKale Center if it were available, but if not, then at a middle school or at a court near the football stadium. Three hundred shots. Over and over.

> ...Over time, the group grew. Junior wing Michael Dickerson joined the freshmen, and then junior guard Miles Simon. One night, Pastner, optimistic by nature, told his teammates that they had no limits.

> ..."Man, I think we can win a national championship," he said, according to Simon's memory.

> ..."Josh, shut up, man, you don't know what you're talking about," Simon replied. "Dude, you're not even going to play. What are you doing?"

> ...Simon didn't realize it then, but he would soon. The 1996-97 Wildcats had something special. A poised freshman

in Bibby. Seasoned vets in Dickerson and Simon. A versatile guard in sophomore Jason Terry.

...."I tell people this all the time: It's the greatest run in the history of the NCAA Tournament," Pastner said with conviction. "It doesn't get enough credit. I don't want to hear about the '85 Villanova team. This run by the Arizona Wildcats in 1997 was the greatest NCAA Tournament run in history."

...Joked Pastner: "I'm the all-time leading rebounder in the history of Arizona."

How many of us would have that kind of optimism and attitude when we weren't playing? How many of us could stay up-beat and help the very teammates that were keeping us from getting playing time? In an article for *Sports Illustrated*, John O'Keefe further highlighted Pastner's team-first attitude and the influence he had on the team's stars,

At his first team meeting, Pastner stood up and preached the value of hard work to All--Pac-10 guard Miles Simon and future NBAers Mike Bibby, Michael Dickerson and Jason Terry. The players laughed. Soon, though, Simon started doing the drills Pastner had recommended to help his stroke. Bibby joined the workouts, and then Terry and forward Bennett Davidson. Says Bibby, now a point guard with the Sacramento Kings, "A lot of those drills I still use today." By season's end, Bibby and Pastner had become roommates.

During his time as a player at Arizona, Hall of Fame coach Lute Olson allowed Pastner to help out with scouting and film break down. He was also in charge of the scout team and continued to push his teammates every day to get better. Here was a guy that started out as a walk-on that became friends with future NBA guys and helped them develop their game even though he was their peer. They valued his maturity and his insights

NEAL BESHEARS LEADS PURDUE

Going into the 2014-15 season, the Purdue University men's basketball team was coming off of a losing season and to make matters worse, they only had one senior. Neal Beshears was the Boilermakers only senior and until coach Matt Painter gave him a scholarship in August of that year, he was also a walk-on.

However, Beshears leadership skills were evident and he played a big part in helping their heralded freshman class transition to college. The Boilermakers won 21 games that year and went to the NCAA Tournament. Combining his playing ability with a hand injury, Beshears only played in one game his senior year, but he was still a valuable leader. Nathan Baird of the *Journal & Courier* wrote about Beshears influence on the team,

> "Most (walk-ons), because they don't play a lot, they're afraid that if they say something, the guys that play a lot aren't going to respond to them," Beshears said. "I think a lot of the guys respect us and respect the walk-ons. If we're doing what we're supposed to it helps us influence them as far as doing the right things and playing the right way."

> …"The walk-ons that we have, they have a lot of knowledge and a lot of good input," sophomore guard Kendall Stephens said. "We as players, we look to that and we accept it and we realize they know what they're talking about. They're great athletes and they can contribute. They're teammates just like us."

> …Over the summer, Beshears and the other walk-ons (Stephen Toyra and Rapheal Davis) organized workouts to help integrate the five incoming freshmen into the Purdue system.

> …Beshears said "Giving them a transition period in the summer where we can teach them, where it's a non-confrontational environment and you don't have any coaches yelling at you and it's a slower pace where they can learn, I think that's going to be a good thing for them."

…"He's been in our program four years and done a good job," Purdue coach Matt Painter said. "He practices hard, he knows what's going on. The guy shows up and plays hard every single day."

…"He's working really hard, whether it be in the weight room or in practice," Davis said. "He's a guy that guys look up to just because of his work ethic. He shows how to work hard.
"I'd rather us win than get playing time," Beshears said. "If that's the trade-off, I'm fine with that."

In an interview with Kyle Rowland of the *Journal Gazette*, Purdue coach Matt Painter had high praise for Beshears and how his influence helped the team be successful when he said about Beshears,

"Neal has been very consistent. He's worked hard. He's quiet so it's hard for him to speak up, but he has. Leadership sometimes is showing up every day, working hard and doing your best. People ultimately respect others who do things the right way and work hard, and he fits into that category."

Anyone can earn the respect of their teammates and coaches by leading themselves. Once you earn this respect, then the sky is the limit in terms of how much influence you have on your teammates. When they respect you, they will listen to you.

7.
POSITIONAL LEADERSHIP

"Being in power is like being a lady. If you have to tell people you are, you aren't."
— **Margaret Thatcher**

"Leadership is extremely important. I tell every team that it's the seniors' team. If they do a good job leading, then we're going to have a great year."
— **Roy Williams**

"Earn your leadership every day."
— **Michael Jordan**

"The ultimate measure of a man is not where he stands in moments of comfort and convenience, but where he stands at times of challenge and controversy."
— **Martin Luther King, Jr.**

"Don't go around saying the world owes you a living; the world owes you nothing; it was here first."
— **Mark Twain**

Even though every player on a team is a leader (either positive or negative), there still is a crucial element of leadership that captains or other positional leaders can provide. Being the team's captain, senior or star is a great opportunity to represent your team in a public manner. It is a great opportunity to create a championship culture that everyone can be proud of. Bill Walsh, the Hall of Fame football coach with the San Francisco 49ers had an interesting take on his positional leaders in his book *The Score Takes Care of Itself* when he said,

> "One of the reasons the 49ers won five Super Bowls in fourteen years is that we expected veterans to everything possible to bring along rookies. In effect, they were expected to train their own replacements, and it was one of the reasons I prohibited hazing. I wanted new players, new staff members, new scouts, and everyone else who joined us to sense immediately they had joined an organization with a unique environment".

You might have positional status on your team but remember that more influence is exerted through personal power than through positional power. However, if you combine positive personal power with positive positional power then you can make a tremendous impact. The stronger that your foundation cove values are and the better habits that you have, then the better you will be able to lead. An old cliché says that in calm waters, every ship has a good captain. As a positional leader, you will be tested when the storms come. If you have developed a strong connection with your teammates and have built up positive daily habits then you will be a calming influence when your team faces challenges.

Your coach and your teammates are going to rely on you. As a positional leader, you should be an individual that your team shouldn't have to worry about. They know that you are going to consistently have the best interests of the team in mind. The coach might set the vision and define the culture for the team but it is the players that will carry it out and make it a reality. As a captain, star or senior, you will be at the center of this. You have a great responsibility to help the team progress and to take ownership in creating a championship culture.

KEVIN DURANT

Kevin Durant is a special talent in the NBA. He is a 6'10" player with Go-Go Gadget arms. He can play any position on the floor. He is a matchup nightmare for opposing coaches. He is too big for guards to handle but too athletic and skilled when bigger players attempt to stop him. Outside of Lebron James, there probably isn't a better basketball player on the planet than KD. He is the epitome of a player that outworks his talent. He has tremendous talent but doesn't rest on that fact. He doesn't stop at talent alone. In fact, his former coach, Scott Brooks, once said of Durant,

"He works and practices like he is trying to make the team."

That is what people say about hard-working blue-collar type role players. That is not often said about the stars. Think about what an average player can do if they out-work everyone. Now think about a star that takes on that same mentality. Durant has gone from being a supremely talented player to a great player.

More importantly, KD wanted to be more than just a great player. He wanted to be a great teammate. Great players who are also great teammates can inspire others to do more and go farther. Durant is a great player, a great teammate and a great champion. After he won the 2013-2014 NBA MVP award (with 119 of 125 possible first-place votes), his acceptance speech gave us a glimpse inside of the mindset that has made him such a great teammate. His speech gave insights into why he is both an MVP player and an MVP leader.

Championships in team sports are won by individuals coming together and playing as a team. Durant understood this. He might be the best player but he still can't do it alone. He plays a team game. That is one reason that he thanks and praises his teammates. He knows that he is talented but he also recognizes the sacrifices of his teammates and how they push and encourage him to be his best.

During his speech, it seemed that Durant thanked everybody in the organization by name. He even mentioned specific things about most of the people that he thanked. When it comes to success, no man is an island and he seemed to understand basketball coach John Wooden's philosophy of

"It takes ten hands to make a basket."

Everybody has a platform. Everybody can influence somebody else through their words or actions. When a star with the platform of a Kevin Durant steps up and provides a positive example then it can affect a number of people. If you are a star, a captain or an upperclassman, you have a bigger responsibility because you have a bigger platform. Will you use your position to add value to others or to prop yourself up? Kevin Durant chose to lift others up. No matter your role, you can inspire others. When you have a position of responsibility, you have an increased opportunity to make a positive impact. One of his most impressive statements was when he said,

"Basketball is just a platform for me to inspire people."

What about you? Does your sport, coaches or teammates exist to serve you? Are you waiting for what you think you are entitled to? Durant isn't like this and he is one of the best players of all-time. He serves others. He wants to inspire others. He wants to use his platform and status for good. You have a choice in everything that you do but in the end, that choice makes you. Will choose to be served by others or will you look for ways to encourage, praise and uplift others like Kevin Durant?

TALENT MUST EXCEED YOUR PROBLEMS

Santonio Holmes was the Pittsburgh Steelers' first-round draft pick in 2006 after playing at Ohio State. He was extremely talented as you had to look no further than his earning MVP honors of Super Bowl XLIII when the Steelers defeated the Arizona Cardinals. So why was he traded by the Steelers that off-season for just a 5th round pick? Probably the same reason that he was out of the NFL entirely five years later. Even though he was talented, his talent did not exceed his problems. In the story on ESPN.com about the breaking trade news, the article described Holmes as the "talented but troubled wide receiver."

Looking back, the Steelers probably did the right thing in getting rid of this locker room problem and selfish, though talented, player before he hurt their organization. In fact, he was suspended for the first four games of the 2010 season for failing the league's drug policy. His history of being a locker room cancer and getting into legal trouble off-the-field probably shortened his career. There was no question that Santonio Holmes' had tremendous talent but his leadership was lacking, which most likely cut short a promising career much earlier than it should have.

One of his most infamous seasons was in 2011 when he was a member of the New York Jets. During that season he criticized coaches, the starting quarterback, and the offensive line. He even fought with teammates in a huddle and was benched during a key game. All of this while he wore the captain "C" on his jersey. Every coach wants their captains to be unafraid to speak up. However, the speaking should be productive and have a point. Holmes seemed to allow his verbal vomit to do nothing but stink things up. He had talent but couldn't keep his mouth shut and didn't help his teammates focus on the important stuff…like winning. He made things about him.

After the 2011 season, he would say that he was unfairly labeled as the scapegoat for the Jets difficult season. As the team captain, a Super Bowl MVP just two years previously and a guy that signed a 5-year, $45-million contract prior to the 2011 season, that would probably qualify him as someone that could have had a huge influence on the team. If he was giving his all on every play and being a respected member of the locker room then he would have been able to help the Jets.

As an athlete, you can learn from Holmes' career. Talent is important but is not the only thing. Are you making your team better in the locker room? Are you adding value to your teammates? Are you staying out of trouble? Are you reliable? Are you focused on the team or your own agenda?

DEREK JETER

In a long line of New York Yankee greats, Derek Jeter is considered by many to be the greatest of all. He ended his career 6th on baseball's all-time hits list and earned the nicknames "Captain Clutch" and "Mr. November" for his success when it mattered most as he led the Yankees to five World Championships. Yes, his play was at a Hall of Fame caliber for 20 years but what was most impressive and has endeared him to fans and foe alike were his leadership skills.

Joe Giglio wrote an article for *Bleacher Report* during Jeter's final 2014 season. In it, we gain some insights into why Jeter was such a good leader and what his teammates thought of him,

Although Jeter wasn't officially named a captain until 2003, it was clear who the leader of the team was from the moment the rookie shortstop began his first full season in 1996.

..."Derek carried himself like a veteran," Dwight "Doc" Gooden said. "Confident, but not cocky. What I always admired about Derek was how he never changed. When I came back to the Yankees in 2000, he was the same exact guy. Much more accomplished and with a big contract, but that work ethic never changed."

...Tino Martinez—a teammate of Jeter's throughout New York's dynasty run from 1996-2001—extolled similar praises and acknowledged that vocal leadership wasn't Jeter's specialty, but it didn't have to be in order to get the mandate across.

..."He led by example," Martinez said. "His whole career has been that way. Plays hard, plays to win. Expects the most from his teammates. When you're in battle with a guy like that, it's important not to let him down. From superstars to the 25th man on the roster, we all felt a responsibility to play hard and play to win because of Jeter. That's rare."

When your best player is also your hardest worker and most respected team member then your chance for on-field success is increased. Just as impressive was how Jeter seemed to stay away from the drama that could have sabotaged his team. He was a celebrity in the nation's biggest city. He dated movie stars and singers. Yet, he was considered the ultimate professional. He had a personal life away from baseball but was wise about it and conducted himself as a professional and did not let it interfere with his play or that of his teammates. If he could be the consummate professional and leader underneath such a large microscope then what is stopping you and your teammates from keeping the drama out of the locker room and staying focused on your goals?

EXAM WITH ONE QUESTION

How you treat people that are below you or don't benefit you at a particular moment says a lot about your character. What is your attitude toward the freshmen, the reserves, the assistant coaches, the trainers, or the walk-ons? Your leadership power can be increased exponentially if you have a greater positive influence on people.

In order to increase this influence, you must be someone that is respected. The more value you add to others, the more others will look to you. Humility is not thinking less of yourself, but rather thinking of yourself less. In other words, how can you think of others more and add more value to them?

In a *NY Times* interview, Walt Bettinger, the Chief Executive of Charles Schwab talked about a major lesson that he learned in college:

"A business strategy course in my senior year stands out. I had maintained a 4.0 average all the way through, and I wanted to graduate with a perfect average. It came down to the final exam, and I had spent many hours studying and memorizing formulas to do calculations for the case studies.

The teacher handed out the final exam, and it was on one piece of paper, which really surprised me because I figured it would be longer than that. Once everyone had their paper, he said, 'Go ahead and turn it over.' Both sides were blank.

And the professor said, 'I've taught you everything I can teach you about business in the last 10 weeks, but the most important message, the most important question, is this: What's the name of the lady who cleans this building?'

And that had a powerful impact. It was the only test I ever failed, and I got the B I deserved. Her name was Dottie, and I didn't know Dottie. I'd seen her, but I'd never taken the time to ask her name. I've tried to know every Dottie I've worked with ever since.

It was just a great reminder of what really matters in life, and that you should never lose sight of people who do the real work."

Ralph Waldo Emerson provided great perspective on this very matter when he said,

"Every man that I meet is in some way my superior and in that way, I learn from him."

Imagine how much can be accomplished and how much you can impact someone else's life for the positive just by thinking about others a little more. What if you were the starting quarterback who got hurt but never took an interest in your backup. The team will suffer because you were only focused on you. Imagine what kind of a reputation you could develop for both you and your team if you did some unselfish things?

QUARTERBACK'S BROKEN JAW
How do you conduct yourself in the locker room? Do you have the team's respect? Going into the 2015 NFL season, Geno Smith was the projected starting quarterback for the New York Jets. They had high hopes as they had a great defense and had some explosive veteran playmakers such as Brandon Marshall and Eric Decker. Smith, the 39th pick of the 2013 draft was highly regarded coming out of West Virginia. The season changed on August 11, 2015, when Smith got into an altercation in the locker room with IK Enemkpali. Smith was punched so hard that his jaw was broken.

The Jets season wouldn't be the same as Smith only appeared in one game during that season. In this one instance, Smith, the team's quarterback did not provide the leadership that the team needed. In this one instance, he didn't appear to know how to get along with at least one teammate and didn't understand his role and responsibility to be above any pettiness. His lack of focus on what was most important for both himself and his team would end up costing the Jets their hopes of a playoff season.

BROTHER GOT IN TROUBLE ON THE BUS.
Basketball was everything to me. It was my number one sport. When I was in 7th grade, I was riding the bus home after school. My brother, who was three years younger than me was acting up quite a bit on the bus that

particular day. He was pestering many kids around him, as well as talking back to the bus driver. Eventually, he would receive a pink slip and be suspended for a time from having bus-riding privileges. I thought it was funny because my annoying little brother got in trouble.

This humor would soon be turned to frustration as my parents told me that I would not be allowed to play in any basketball games while my brother was suspended from the bus. They told me that I was brother's keeper and could have kept him from getting in trouble. I thought that this was unfair. However, they were right in the fact I could have stopped this. My little brother looked up to me and I could have influenced him and deescalated the situation. I wasn't trying to do the right thing or make a positive impact, I was just being mean and not helping the situation

THE TRAVEL BAG

When you are the captain or best player on the team, more people will watch you based upon your positional leadership. Everyone can be a leader because everyone can have influence, however, if you have positional leadership then you automatically have a larger scope of influence. Alan Williams was a walk-on at Wake Forest University a few years after Tim Duncan graduated. The new star was Robert O'Kelley, who ended up being a Top-10 scorer in Wake Forest history. In Williams' book "Walk On", he told a great story of O'Kelley that highlights how a positional leader can have a positive influence on his teammates

In the book, Williams recalls how everyone got a brand new Nike travel bag except for the walk-on. However, when the player came into the locker room after practice, there was a bag in Williams locker. The stitching on the page said #4, which was O'Kelley's number. Everyone can be a leader because everyone can influence somebody else. However, if you have someone in a position of leadership like Robert O'Kelley then you have increased opportunities to make a larger impact.

I PAID MY DUES

I once took over a team that had some seniors that were very talented but also subscribed to the traditional philosophy of leadership in that seniors, especially senior starters should be served. They had "paid their dues" in the past and now it was time for others to pay their dues. During the preseason, our travel suits arrived but unfortunately the vendor had messed up and sent some incorrect sizes.

The replacement travel suits would arrive a few days later. We were not playing games yet and picture day was still a few weeks away. We would be doing no team functions that required the team to dress uniformly. Since they would be only wearing them around campus and it would only be a couple of days anyways, I decided to make sure that the freshmen had the proper sizes since they didn't have any travel suits. This would mean that some of the seniors would go without a new travel suit for a couple of days.

I explained my rationale to them but unfortunately, one of the seniors vehemently disagreed with the decision and ended up quitting the next day. This player was the top-returning scorers and she had said that she had "paid her dues" and no freshmen should get something before she did. Not only did she fail to grasp the idea of servant leadership and thinking about the team, but she also demonstrated a lack of respect toward others. In most situations, if you want respect, then you must first, be worthy of that respect and second, be willing to give it.

JACKIE ROBINSON

Many of you have probably seen the move *42* depicting Jackie Robinson's life. Jackie Robinson was the first African-American to play major-league baseball when he suited up for the Brooklyn Dodgers in 1947. There is a scene in the movie that actually happened in real life, though there is some debate as to whether it happened when the movie said that it did according to an ESPN.com article by Brian Cronin. Regardless, it is a great story of how a person's influence can make a difference.

In breaking the color barrier, Robinson faced all kinds abuse, both physically and verbally. One day when the Dodgers were playing at home, he committed an error while playing second base. The crowd began to get nasty. Even his own fans were being rude and loud. All of a sudden, Brooklyn's short stop Pee Wee Reese came over to Jackie and put his arm around him. Reese was a beloved Dodger and the fans couldn't bring themselves to ridicule him. The fans stopped booing and yelling. Robinson would later say that the moment Reese stood next to him was the day his career was saved. Reese would later say,

> "I was just trying to make the world a little bit better. That's what you're supposed to do with your life, isn't it?"

If you are a player that is in a positional role (captain, senior, starter), imagine how much influence you can have on your team and those around you. Your words and actions are powerful. You might never do something as monumental as Pee Wee Reese did for Jackie Robinson, but you can still use your positional authority to improve whatever situation you find yourself in.

TOM BRADY

Celebrating and sharing successes with your teammates in a great way to earn their respect and increase your potential for influence. There is no question that Tom Brady is the on-field leader of the New England Patriots. Arguably the greatest quarterback in NFL history, Brady seems to understand that the Patriots prolonged dominance is not just because of an accurate arm, quick decision-making skills or ability to elude rushers. The quarterback is almost always the on-field leader because of their position. Every team in America has a starting quarterback, however, not every team has a true person of influence at that position.

When the New England Patriots went 16-0 during the 2007 regular season, Brady gave each of his starting offensive linemen Audi SUVs. Later on, he made headlines when he won a truck for earning the Super Bowl 49 MVP award but subsequently gave the prize to defensive back Malcolm Butler, whose pass break up on the final play sealed the victory. He even has done things midseason for the entire team. In 2016, he gave every teammate a pair of Uggs after the eighth game of the season.

Talent is just one part of being a team leader. A quarterback that doesn't have the respect of his teammates will never be able to maximize their physical abilities. You want to have enough time to find open receivers then you better be a person whose linemen care enough about to protect.

Oftentimes, the easiest way to get respect is to get respect. Celebrate the successes of others. Tom Brady has learned through the years how to celebrate and share his success with others. Individuals who excel in team sports can't do it alone. Brady understands this.

HEAVY LIFTING

The best leaders are also very good at serving. Dr. Martin Luther Kind once said,

"Everybody can be great because anybody can serve."

To serve just means to render assistance, be of use or to help in some way. It doesn't mean that you are less than somebody else. It just means that you are helpful. Here is a story from the American Revolutionary War that highlights this premise of serving,

Many years ago during the Revolutionary War, a rider on horseback came across a group of soldiers under the command of a corporal who was out to show he was in charge.

They were building a tall log fortification alongside a road and the corporal kept barking orders. Trying with all their might to push the final log in place up top, they couldn't do it. Every time the last log would come crashing down. The corporal would shout out again, "Up with it! Push harder! What's your problem?"

Once more they would attempt to give it the heave-ho and lift the last log only to have the log fall again. Dismounting his horse, the stranger carefully took his place alongside the soldiers.

"Now, all together boys – heave!" he said. And the big piece of timber slid into place.

Before the men could thank the stranger, he got back on his horse.

The quiet man asked the corporal, "Why didn't you help your men with the heavy lifting?"

He said, "Don't you see? I'm a corporal!"

The stranger replied, "Pardon me. I didn't realize that you were so important."

He then opened up his coat revealing his uniform, and he said, "I am just a mere Commander-in Chief. George Washington, at your service Corporal. The next time you have a log too heavy for your men to lift, send for me!"

George Washington was a great leader because he wasn't afraid of serving. He was willing to do some heavy lifting. The best leaders are servants. Servant leaders don't focus on rank or position. When they serve, they are not thinking about their rank. They are just trying to help.

CAPTAIN'S LETTER
One of the best books that I have ever read that is applicable for both coaches and players is Dick Devenzio's *Runnin' the Show*. It contains hundreds of practical tips and insights to help improve players and a team. One of the sections deals with leadership and captains. Dick Devenzio was the top-rated guard in the country coming out of high school before becoming an all-conference player in the ACC for Duke University in the 1970's. After his playing days were over, he founded the Point Guard College, which is genuinely regarded as the top instructional basketball camp in the country. In the book, Devenzio published a letter from a player at a small school in Oregon. This is a good example of what you can do for your team if you are in a positional leadership role:

To the Future Linfield National Champions Hoops Team,

"He is no fool who gives what he cannot keep to gain what he cannot lose." (Jim Elliott)

I hope that your two months of vacation time have been the best ever. As for me, I have been working my tail off looking forward to our upcoming season. Six days ago

Aaron Lee and I began lifting and shooting for (around) two hours a day. (My position of head toilet cleaner on campus has given me the wonderful privilege of gym key use).

Summer for all of you should be over. It's time to begin paying the price for a National Championship, for which the cost is not a small one. We need to be putting more time in than any other team in the nation. We have the talent, we have the character, all we have to do is now pay the price in the weight room, on the court, and in our minds.

"Anything the mind can conceive and believe, it can achieve." (Larry Southers)

Do you believe that we can win the NC baby? What are you doing to match your beliefs? If you truly believe that we can win the National Championship, your life will be changed.

Work out at top speed, push yourself beyond anything you have ever known, and dream of the days to come.

The only thing that we lack to this point right now is playing together and knowing each other, which is a big ingredient to being a championship caliber team. In order to offset this problem, we are going to have to be very exclusive in our play. To win big, we must sacrifice big. I have gone ahead and made some preliminary plans for the fall and I would like to bounce them off you guys as soon as the school year starts.

The varsity team will be meeting at Coach Doty's house the first three days of school - Wednesday, Thursday, Friday - for BBQ's up there to go over our fall game plan and pre-season discussion. Begin putting time in now with extra running, shooting, and lifting so that we can get a phat jump on becoming the first National Championship team Linfield hoops has ever had.

God bless all you guys. I look forward to seeing you soon.

Dy #23

What a great letter. If you are in a position of leadership, have you sent a note, letter, email or Facebook message to your teammates inspiring them for the upcoming season? The coach can only do so much but when a positional leader takes on a role of key influencer then the sky is the limit. Coaches want players to step up and make suggestions that make sense. I bet that Matt's coach loved that he took initiative and was committed to making his team as good as it could be. What are you doing to be the best leader and captain that you can be?

8.
VERBAL LEADERSHIP

"I can say through 40 years of NFL experience that leadership comes in a lot of shapes and sizes. I've had players who were very vocal that were great leaders. I've had players who were vocal that weren't great leaders. It's not about volume or who's the most talkative guy. It's the guy who does his job and puts the best interest of the team and organization in the lead."
– Bill Belichick

"What you do is what you believe. Everything else is just talk."
– Denny Lehnus

"You have to hold people accountable. You're not always going to be the most popular. If you want to win, sometimes you have to have a difficult conversation with people. You know they are not going to like you. But you do it because you want what is best for the team."
– Carla Overbeck

"Wise men speak because they have something to say; Fools speak because they have to say something."
– Plato

"On good teams, coaches hold players accountable. On great teams, players hold each other accountable."
– Joe Dumars

One of the most common leadership myths is that some leaders are vocal and some lead by example. Remember that leadership is about influence. All student-athletes are people of influence through both their actions and their words. You can't just tell people what to do and expect to be a verbal leader without being a leader by example.

Words with the action to back them up are hollow at best and hypocritical at worst. The main misconception related to this deals with players that say that they are not verbal leaders. This is simply not true. If you can talk, you can lead verbally. Players talk all day long. Players have influence all day long. What is true is that you might not be a rah-rah, intense verbal leader like a Ray Lewis, Tim Tebow or Lebron James. You don't have to be loud and vocal unless you have a position of leadership or you are the most logical person to say what needs to be said at that particular time.

However, every player should be leading verbally. You should always be providing a kind word of encouragement. You should always be sticking up for wrong on the team (e.g. when a teammate is picking on another teammate) if you have a relationship with that person. Speaking of that, if you do not have a strong connection of trust with a teammate then your verbal influence will be limited. For instance, if a teammate is slacking and you point it out publicly without that strong connection then it could actually do more harm than good. When you confront someone or try to hold a teammate accountable, you must have some trust built up. There must be a relationship that exists where that person will have a reason to listen to you.

If this is the case, you are probably close to a teammate that is close to that person. You might be able to talk with the other teammate about the situation and influence them to step up as a verbal leader behind the scenes. Your goal should be to maintain unity on the team and keep all the players moving forward toward your common objective. If a player feels that you are embarrassing them in front of others, it will create additional challenges for your team.

Teammates need to know that you care about them and that they can trust you. You must choose your words carefully and the appropriate timing. Most leadership happens behind closed doors in much smaller settings. Most influence occurs where a connection has been made. The great generals Robert E. Lee and Napoleon were known for asking their soldiers about their families and knowing them personally before going into battle. They were successful on the battlefield, not only because of their military prowess but because they connected with their men.

The type of motivation that you see in movies like Braveheart and the Gladiator is rare. The rah-rah fired up speeches are a short-term inspiration. Long-lasting influence is when people know, like and trust you. When a relationship is present then successful verbal influence can take place. Having a friendship or building a connection sometimes takes work. It is an intentional act by you to value another person. Here are a few ideas on how to connect with others more effectively:

1. Don't be afraid to apologize first.
2. Do a favor for them without expecting anything in return.
3. Give a gift for no reason.
4. A hand-written note of encouragement or thanks.
5. Take them out for coffee/lunch and make it about them (ask questions).
6. Be encouraging and supportive.
7. Be respectfully honest (accountability)
8. Have their well-being in mind.
9. Only give the unsolicited advice if it absolutely necessary (detrimental to them, someone else or the team).
10. Don't be petty. Likewise, don't get offended by stupid petty stuff.

TIM TEBOW

In 2008, the University of Florida football team was undefeated and ranked #4 nationally. They were playing at home against Ole Miss, who was unranked and 2-2. In a huge upset, Ole Miss defeated the Gators 31-30. After the game, Heisman Trophy winner and Florida quarterback Tim Tebow took to the podium and, not only apologized for his performance but also made a promise that would become legendary. The Gators proceeded to win 10 games in a row, including a 24-14 win against Oklahoma in the National Championship game. Here are Tebow's words from that Ole Miss press conference, which has become known simply as "The Promise",

"To the fans and everybody in Gator Nation, I'm sorry. I'm extremely sorry. We were hoping for an undefeated season. That was my goal, something Florida has never done here. I promise you one thing, a lot of good will come out of this. You will never see any player in the entire country play as hard as I will play the rest of the season. You will never see someone push the rest of the team as hard as I will push everybody the rest of the season. You will never see a team play harder than we will the rest of the season. God Bless."

The very next year, coach Urban Meyer put up a plaque outside the Florida football complex so that all visiting fans and all players entering can see the facility would be reminded of this leadership by Tebow and the accomplishment of the team. Certainly, this is an extreme case of verbal leadership. Not everyone is able to say these things and fewer still are able to back it up. But Tebow took that opportunity to motivate his teammates – and himself!

Once he said this stuff publicly, then he had to back it up both in his play and the way that he added value to his teammates. Football is the ultimate team sport. As good as Tebow was, he knew that he needed his teammates to perform at a high level to achieve their championship goals. In order to back up his words, he had to encourage and influence his teammates to perform at their highest level.

ACCOUNTABILITY

In Patrick Lencioni's best-selling book *The Five Dysfunction of a Team*, Dysfunction #4 is Avoidance of Accountability. This is important because a team that avoids accountability with one another creates resentment among team members who have different standards of performance. It can also encourage mediocrity, which means you are the best of the bad. With mediocrity, you are as close to the bottom as you are the top. The other key problem with no accountability with team members is that it places an undue burden on the team leader (normally the coach or captain) as the sole source of discipline.

The most successful teams – those with championship cultures – have team members that are willing to hold each other accountable in the appropriate ways. Accountability works both ways. Players have to be willing to confront in a positive way but other players have to be coachable, willing to listen and make the appropriate changes. Your coaches can't be the only ones holding players accountable. If this is happening then your coaches are going to get worn out and not be as sharp with preparing your team for games and practices.

Secondly, they are not in the dorm rooms, car rides to and from practice, cafeteria, or locker rooms with you. They don't know everything that is going on. If the off-court standards are not being handled by team members then they may not be handled at all and will turn into major issues that derail your team from achieving its' goals.

WHAT SHOULD I SAY TO MY TEAMMATES?

There are two occasions when you will talk with your teammates – normal friend talk and sport related talk. Most players know how to talk with their friends. The sport-related talk is a little trickier but it still comes back to the common fundamentals of communication of respect, trust, honesty, and tact. Here are 3 situations in which you would be verbal with teammates in a sport-related manner…

> **Encouraging** – You should always be looking for ways to encourage your teammates. This could be in the form of reminding them of something like "Next Play". This is a phrase that Duke basketball and Coach K made famous that serves as a reminder that they can move on even if they just messed up. You can refocus your teammate with an encouraging word. You can provide energy and inspire the team like the example of Monmouth's bench in chapter 6. Your encouraging words can be in private or public. Both are useful. When you do it publicly, other players may catch on. Enthusiasm is contagious.

> **Informative** – This might be reminding base runners what the situation is in softball (e.g. "two outs, running on anything") or football players relaying the play in a huddle. It might be letting your teammates know that coach just changed up plans and you will be meeting in the weight room first before practice. It could be reminding two of

your teammates that all three of you have bus cleanup duty when you get back to school. Anyone can pass on accurate information in an appropriate manner. During a game or practice, you might yell "help side" or "watch the linebacker" or "shooter in the corner" – things that help your teammates.

Accountability – Holding your teammates accountable is typically the toughest type of verbal leadership but it can be the most crucial. Allowing behaviors to go unchecked or standards to be unmet, is the quickest way to develop a losing culture. It is best to confront people that you have a good relationship with and do it in an appropriate way. For instance, calling out someone in front of the team should probably be reserved as a last resort. Sometimes, an encouraging reminder can proactively minimize the need for confrontation later (e.g. "Come on guys, we got this sprint. Let's all make our time and we will be done. It's just like the last defensive possession of a game. Let's win this game.")

MAYA MOORE
Maya Moore is one of the most-decorated basketball players of all-time. She was a two-time college player of the year while a member of the UCONN dynasty. In the WNBA, she has led the Minnesota Lynx to championships in 2011, 2013 and 2015 after entering the league as a rookie in 2011. She is extremely well-respected.

Moore understands her responsibility as a star player but she used to be a quiet leader. Moore once said,

> "I want to be a shining light and bring life to every situation."

Phil Ervin wrote an article for *Fox Sports* that talked about Moore understanding the need for her to be more vocal and here are a few excerpts from that,

"The way she sets an example on the floor is one thing, and then she's always talking to you," said Tricia Liston, the 12th overall pick in the April 14 draft. "She's trying to help you. She's telling you 'do this, do that.' If you mess up a little bit, she's gonna tell you how to do it the best way."

..."The very first time we circled up (after practice) with this group, Maya had tremendous things to offer," Lynx coach Cheryl Reeve said. "It's just been nonstop since then, that she just really, really understands the value of her words."

...Said Maya Moore: "It's definitely an opportunity for me to step up and just do the things that I've been taught to do growing up . . . just constantly being someone who is vocally engaged.

..."She's always going 100 percent," Liston said. "Yesterday in a drill that I don't even know if we were going 100 percent, she's diving on the floor trying to get her stops."

Moore wasn't always a verbal leader but she is learning to be. It is never too late to become a better leader. Sometimes that means stepping up your game in an area that isn't as comfortable. Just like you sometimes have to work extra hard on developing a skill (e.g. dribbling with your left hand), you also have to develop another area of your leadership game.

CHICAGO BULLS
Talented teams can self-destruct when they cannot lead themselves. A lack of leadership with a team derails more teams than a lack of talent. Most teams have players that can play. The best teams have players that can positively lead.

In 2016, the Chicago Bulls had high hopes with the acquisitions of future Hall of Famer Dwyane Wade and Rajon Rondo, who led the NBA in assists the previous year. These two were supposed to join up with rising superstar Jimmy Butler. Instead, a lack of leadership derailed the team's potential. Sure, they made the playoffs as the last seed and with a 41-41 record. This was a far cry from what they were expecting with a talented roster.

Butler and Wade, the team's top two scorers were fined by the team for making comments. A portion of Wade's comments included the following,

> "I'm 35 years old, man. I've got three championships. It shouldn't hurt me more than it hurts these young guys. They have to want it. ... It has to change. It has to hurt inside to lose games like this."

Butler then echoed Wade's remarks, saying:

> "(Expletive teammates) just got to care if we win or lose. At the end of the day, do whatever it takes to help the team win. You play your role to the T. Be a star in your role, man."

I can't speak to whether they were right in their assessment about their teammates but I do know that leadership begins with each individual. Did they do all that they could do? They are the two stars of the team. As Gandhi said, "be the change that you want to see in the world." Did they provide positive guidance to their other teammates? Did they provide a positive example? Were they showing the way to the other Bulls and helping them maximize their potential or were they just relying on their status and past successes as the reason people should follow them?

Evidently, there was some animosity toward Butler and Wade from other players on the team because the veteran Rondo, the team's leader in assists took to Instagram to voice his opinion of the team's two stars and compared them to his former World Championship teammates during his Boston Celtic days,

> "My vets would never go to the media. They would come to the team. My vets didn't pick and choose when they wanted to bring it. They brought it every time they stepped in the gym whether it was practice or a game. They didn't take days off. My vets didn't care about their numbers. My vets played for the team. When we lost, they wouldn't blame us. They took responsibility and got in the gym. They showed the

young guys what it meant to work. Even in Boston when we had the best record in the league, if we lost a game, you could hear a pin drop on the bus. They showed us the seriousness of the game. My vets didn't have an influence on the coaching staff. They couldn't change the plan because it didn't work for them. I played under one of the greatest coaches, and he held everyone accountable. It takes 1-15 to win. When you isolate everyone, you can't win consistently. I may be a lot of things, but I'm not a bad teammate. My goal is to pass what I learned along. The young guys work. They show up. They don't deserve blame. If anything is questionable, it's the leadership."

Wow, shots fired! Rondo probably had a point but this should not have been aired publicly. This should have happened behind closed doors. More importantly, Rondo completely missed the point of what he is saying.

He was a veteran on the team and was not doing what he said his veterans should have been doing. When he said that his vets would never go to the media, I guess he didn't consider Instagram as a media outlet. I guess when he said that he wasn't a bad teammate, he was overlooking the fact that he was criticizing other teammates publicly – no matter how justified. If his goal was to truly pass along what he had learned then what exactly was he passing along? It was not okay to act that way.

I am guessing that none of the Bulls have read Tobias Fredberg's article in *The Harvard Business* Review entitled "Why Good Leaders Pass the Cred and Take the Blame" in which he says,

> "They [leaders] see the willingness to accept personal responsibility — especially during tough times — as critical to winning the trust of employees and other stakeholders. Leaders, in their view, need the endurance and stamina to lead their organizations through thick and thin. They also need to contain the anxiety of their employees. A leader who spreads the blame, who fails to accept that he or she is ultimately the one in charge, increases the insecurity of their people and lessens the likelihood that they'll take ownership of initiatives."

So what was the takeaway from this incident? Good leaders help make others better. They don't point out flaws in public.

Good leaders are not hypocrites. You can't take a stand saying that someone else is being a bad leader while demonstrating that very same behavior.

Good leaders earn respect daily. The best way to earn respect is to be trusted. The best way to be trusted is to build a connection with others. This does not happen if you are tearing them down publicly.

Good leaders are not concerned about their egos or getting their own way or their stats or how they look in the media. Good leaders care about their teammates.

Good leaders recognize that it is a team effort. Jimmy Butler said the players need to be stars in their roles. Butler, Wade, and Rondo needed to heed this advice. Their roles extended far beyond scoring or passing. As leaders, their role was to know the way, show the way and go the way. They might have filled up the stat sheet but their lack of leadership led the Bulls to a .500 record and being bounced in the first round of the NBA playoffs.

9.

TEAMWORK

"Coming together is a beginning.
Keeping together is progress.
Working together is success."
– Henry Ford

"The main ingredient to stardom is the rest of the team."
– John Wooden

"Your team doesn't care if you are a super star. They care if
you are a super teammate."
– Jon Gordon

"You can do what I cannot do. I can do what you cannot do.
Together we can do great things."
– Mother Teresa

"The greatest compliment to any player is he's a great
teammate. We can't all be great players but we can all be great
teammates."
– Jay Bilas

The old acronym of T.E.A.M in which together everyone achieves more is true more often than not. Players need teammates that are willing and able to do the things that they can't or don't want to do. We all have strengths and weaknesses. Just like the strength of each wolf is the wolfpack and the strength of the wolfpack is each individual wolf, so it is on teams. Each team has players with different strengths and weaknesses. The best teams have players that understand that they all fit together like a puzzle. Even the most talented softball pitcher can't strike out every batter. They need competent fielders to make plays in the field when the batter hits the ball. A talented outside hitter in volleyball knows that their skills are not maximized if they don't have a good setter.

A team-first mentality and understanding of how crucial every member of a team can be to achieving a common goal is a must in utilizing your leadership potential. The more you respect and praise the various roles on a team, the greater your opportunity for influence will be.

THE TEAM! THE TEAM! THE TEAM!

Regardless of whether you are a fan of the Michigan Wolverines, Ohio State Buckeyes or the Alabama Crimson Tide, you can appreciate the importance of teamwork and how it is crucial for your favorite team to play in an important bowl game or contend for a championship. Bo Schembechler played football at Miami of Ohio for the legendary Woody Hayes. He would also be an assistant coach for Hayes at Ohio State.

When Schembechler took over as head coach at the University of Michigan, he and Hayes embarked on a fierce rivalry that came to be known as the "Ten-Year War." Overall, Schembechler ended his college career with a 234-65-8 record. He ended his career as an athletic director at Michigan and then president of the Detroit Tigers. Schembechler was a fiery coach known for his motivational speeches. One of his most popular has come to be known as "The Team The Team The Team" and it is a good reminder of how special it is to be a part of a team,

"We want the Big Ten championship and we're gonna win it as a Team. They can throw out all those great backs, and great quarterbacks, and great defensive players,

111

throughout the country and in this conference, but there's gonna be one Team that's gonna play solely as a Team.

No man is more important than The Team. No coach is more important than The Team. The Team, The Team, The Team, and if we think that way, all of us, everything that you do, you take into consideration what effect does it have on my Team? Because you can go into professional football, you can go anywhere you want to play after you leave here. You will never play for a Team again. You'll play for a contract. You'll play for this. You'll play for that. You'll play for everything except the team, and think what a great thing it is to be a part of something that is The Team.

We're gonna win it. We're gonna win the championship again because we're gonna play as a team, better than anybody else in this conference, we're gonna play together as a team. We're gonna believe in each other, we're not gonna criticize each other, we're not gonna talk about each other, we're gonna encourage each other. And when we play as a team, when the old season is over, you and I know, it's gonna be Michigan again, Michigan."

EVERY ROLE IS IMPORTANT

What kind of role do you have on your team right now? Are you happy with your role? Maybe you are the team's star or maybe you are "just a role player". Whenever you start to think that you are the most important person on the team or, unfortunately, that you are not important because your role is not glamorous, then think about cars.

Think about the most beautiful car with a big strong engine. Now think about what happens to that shiny fast car that gets everyone's attention if the spark plug is faulty. A $100,000 car can be sidelined by a bad spark plug that costs $10. Cars need all the parts working together properly for them to operate effectively. It is the same with teams. No role is more important than another. Here is a story that Kevin Templeton told in his book *To The Hilt* that really drives this point home in an unforgettable way,

Charlie Plumb graduated from the US Naval Academy. He was a fighter pilot who helped start the "Top Gun" school in Miramar, California. He flew seventy-five missions in F-4 and F-14 Tomcat Phantom jets over Hanoi off the USS Kitty Hawk.

On his seventy-fifth mission, just five days before he was to rotate off active duty, Plumb's plane was hit by a surface-to-air missile. The plane was on fire and would not respond. The stick was frozen. Finally, Charlie and his radar man ejected from the F-4 and parachuted, to be captured by angry North Vietnamese soldiers. Captain Plumb spent almost six years the Hanoi Hilton, a notoriously tough prison. There he faced torture, hunger, filth, and oppressive jungle heat. he went into prison at twenty-four years of age and was released at age thirty after a prisoner exchange.

Charlie was eating dinner at a Kansas City restaurant when a guy a couple of tables over was staring at him. The stranger got up and approached Charlie's table. he said, "You're Charlie Plumb. You flew seventy-four successful missions off the USS Kitty Hawk. On your seventy-fifth mission, you were shot down over Hanoi and captured. You spent six years as a POW at the Hanoi Hilton. You got out when they had a prisoner exchange."

Charlie told the man that he was right. But there were hundreds of men on that ship. An aircraft carrier is huge. It's like a floating city. He was sorry, but he didn't remember the stranger. "Who are you?" he asked.

"I'm the man who packed your parachute," the man answered. Charlie thanked him for doing his job well. He asked him if he knew how many parachutes he had packed. The man said, "No, I never counted. I was just glad I had the opportunity to serve."

Think about that for a moment. The famous and glamorous fighter pilot was saved because an ordinary unknown guy packed his parachute correctly on that particular mission. Can you imagine if the parachute packer had felt sorry for himself because of his lowly job? What if he resented going to work that day because he wanted to be a fighter pilot? What if he wanted to wear the fancy uniform and sunglasses and get all of the attention? What if he had said to himself, 'what does it matter, if a pilot gets shot down, they probably won't survive anyways?'

Parachute packers weren't famous and they didn't get any glory. They sound a little bit like basketball players that set screens, softball players that lay down sacrifice bunts, or football players that block. However, a team cannot be successful without these people. The media will highlight the player that scores the points but will rarely talk about the people that help make those points possible.

If you are a "parachute packer" on your team, then take inspiration from this story. True, your role won't include saving someone's life but it certainly entails helping your team win. Whatever parachute you are asked to pack for your team, do it with the attitude of knowing that, though unglamorous, it is every bit as important for your team's success.

If you are like Charlie Plumb and you are a pilot on your team. If you are a star, then understand that you are not the only important person on the team. Legendary hall of fame basketball coach John Wooden used to say that it takes ten hands to make a basket. Be the first one to high-five the parachute packers on your team. Be the first one to praise them during an interview after the game.

Charlie Plumb, a star pilot, owed his life to a role player that was a star in his role – a role player that took pride in his role regardless of whether he would ever be recognized for it. If Charlie Plumb had died that day, no one would have blamed the parachute packer. All eyes would have been on what the pilot could have done better. Just like in a basketball game, no one notices a bad screen being set or when a pass is a little off target but they do see the shot being missed. If you are in a team sport, it takes every player to do their job in order to achieve success.

CRAB MENTALITY
The opposite of adding value to your teammates is that of having a crab

mentality. The following story highlights the crab principle, which can be true in both sports and in life.

A man was walking along the beach and saw another man fishing in the surf with a bait bucket beside him. As he drew closer, he saw that the bait bucket had no lid and had live crabs inside.

"Why don't you cover your bait bucket so the crabs won't escape?", he said.

"You don't understand.", the man replied, "If there is one crab in the bucket it would surely crawl out very quickly. However, when there are many crabs in the bucket, if one tries to crawl up the side, the others grab hold of it and pull it back down so that it will share the same fate as the rest of them."

When you have a crab mentality, you are only out for yourself. You are going to "get yours" or "play your game." If individuals are not working as a team and are refusing to help one another other out, then a crab mentality is taking place.

OLD WARWICK

When you take a shot in basketball, it probably makes you feel more confident if you know that your teammates will go and rebound the shot if you miss. If you are playing baseball and the hit-and-run play is on, you will feel better as a base runner if you know that the batter swings and makes contact with the ball. If you are a quarterback in football, you want to know that the offensive lineman will be protecting your blindside. Here is a little story about accomplishing more as a team courtesy of coach Shane Dreiling from his blog *Life Lessons in Words*,

> A man became lost while driving through the country. As he tried to read a map, he accidentally drove off the road into a ditch. Though he wasn't injured, his car was stuck deep in the mud. Seeing a farmhouse just down the road, the man walked over to ask for help.

> "Warwick can get you out of the ditch," the farmer said, pointing to an old mule standing in the field. The man looked at the haggard mule, and then looked at the farmer, who just stood there nodding. "Yep, old Warwick can do

the job."

The man figured he had nothing to lose, so the two men and Warwick made their way back to the ditch.

After the farmer hitched the old mule to the car, he snapped the reins and shouted, "Pull, Fred! Pull, Jack! Pull Ted! Pull, Warwick!" With very little effort, the lone mule pulled the car from the ditch.

The man was amazed. He thanked the farmer, patted the mule, and asked, "Why did you call out all those other names before you called Warwick?"

The farmer grinned and said, "Old Warwick is just about blind. As long as he believes he is part of a team, he doesn't mind pulling."

When we play sports, we know that we need others in order to experience the most amount of success. When we play together, we are able to accomplish more. A play works better when all the team members do their jobs.

ENERGY VAMPIRES

Jon Gordon has written a number of best-sellers on leadership, personal growth, and teamwork. In one of his books, *The Energy Bus*, the main characters are discussing a part of teamwork that is crucial to success. You have choices every day whether you are going to add value to others or look out for yourself only. Are you going to be positive or negative? Are you going to encourage others and energize your team or will you suck the life out of them,

> "You asked about the negative people and I'm going to be straight up with you, George. This rule is not for the faint of heart. It's not easy to deal with the negativity in the world but it's something that's got to be done. Your success and life are so important that you must surround yourself with a

positive support team. No one creates success in a vacuum and the people we surround ourselves with have a big influence on the life and success we create.

If you want to be successful you have to be very careful about who is on your bus. After all, there are people who increase your energy and there are people who drain your energy. I call the people who drain your energy Energy Vampires and they will suck the life out of you and your goals and vision if you let them. They will cause an engine leak, make your ride miserable, or even worse slash your tires.

But remember, George, don't take it personal. They are just part of the negativity that exists in the world. Your job is to do your best to eliminate any negativity on your bus and this includes negative people, no matter who they are. This is rule #6 and it's big time."

If you are ever in a position to have a say in who your teammates will be, try to avoid energy vampires at all costs. If you are a college player and have a bad feel about one of your recruits, then let your coach know of your concerns. If you have a teammate already that is an energy vampire then do all within your power to counteract their negativity with your own positivity.

Enthusiasm is contagious. People will oftentimes gravitate toward your positive attitude because it is refreshing and respected. If you have a strong relationship with the energy vampire then try to talk with them at an appropriate time to let them know how this might be affecting the team. Even though enthusiasm is contagious, sometimes negativity can be also if left unchecked.

REDWOOD TREES

If you have been to California, you might have seen the world's biggest trees, the sequoia redwoods. Redwoods grow hundreds of feet in the air, with the tallest rising nearly 300 feet above the ground. These trees survive for thousands of years even when floods, strong winds, earthquakes or fire come their way. The way that they are able to do that is because of their root system. Amazingly, their roots don't go down very far but they spread out up to 100 feet from the tree. As they spread out, they get mixed up with the roots from their neighbors.

Essentially, these trees support one another, not only from the elements but also in sharing water and other nutrients crucial to survival. This strong foundation and interconnectedness allow the redwoods to survive and thrive even in the harshest of conditions. The example of the redwoods is a great illustration for our teams and what a healthy team looks like.

To have a functional and successful team, you must have members that hold each other up, work together and share in each other's strengths to hide weaknesses. Just like the redwoods, our team can be stronger together than we are individually. Even though a redwood is the world's largest tree, without the support of its' neighbors, it would not last very long. The most talented players don't achieve sustained success without the help of their teammates.

DETROIT PISTONS

Many NBA championships have been won by teams with talent that was superior to their opponents. Most casual fans can name the stars on NBA Championships of the past – Michael Jordan and the Bulls, Steph Curry with Golden State, Lebron and the Cavs and Heat, Kobe and Shaq with the Lakers, Tim Duncan with the Spurs and Hakeem Olajuwon with the Houston Rockets. However, there is a team that is often forgotten and hard to identify a star player because they were a true team. They might be skipped over in the talk of greatest teams ever but they all have championship rings and can call themselves "Champions."

The Goin' to Work Pistons won the NBA Title in 2004 when they defeated the Lakers. They then followed it up with another finals appearance the next year when they narrowly lost to the San Antonio Spurs in seven games.

Ben Wallace was the NBA's Defensive Player of the Year four times and he said this in a Keith Langlois article on *NBA.com*,

> "I don't think there are too many teams in any sport that ever won a championship with a team like we had. Guys that

truly cared about each other and didn't care who scores as long as the points were going up on the board, don't care who's getting the stops as long as they're not scoring."

Their mantra and visual that they relied upon was that of an iron fist — five fingers coming together and becoming one iron fist, rather than five individual fingers. Though the starting five of Ben Wallace, Rasheed Wallace, Rip Hamilton, Tayshaun Prince and Chauncey Billups were all accomplished individual players in the NBA, they were better together than they were individually. The whole was greater than the sum of the individual parts. They all had a chip on their shoulder of overcoming obstacles in the NBA. They all had something to prove and instead of proving it on their own, they became one unit focused on a common goal. In the same article, the point guard, Chauncey Billups gave his opinion on one of the reasons they were such a good team when he said,

> "We all literally became brothers. People say that. It's a good cliché, but it was real with us. It was real. Maybe I'm biased, but I don't ever see that happening like we did it. I think that's the last time it'll happen like that."

They might not have had superstars but they had talented players that meshed together. The Goin' to Work Pistons might not have been the five best players in the NBA but they were the best five that you could put together in 2004.

ANDRE IGUADOLA

All players say that they want to win but their actions and attitude may say something different when they actually have to demonstrate this. Andre Iguodala was a star player for the Philadelphia 76ers and Denver Nuggets. He averaged 15.1 points, 5.8 rebounds and 4.9 assists per game in his first nine seasons with the Philadelphia 76ers and the Denver Nuggets. During those nine years, he was oftentimes the star player as he took 11.5 shots per game.

In fact, one of the most impressive things from Iguodala's career was that he started all 695 regular season games. Outside of his rookie season, he never played fewer than 34 minutes per game. He might not have been a

Kobe Bryant or Lebron James, but he was a NBA star. However, Iguodola wanted more – not more points, shots or playing time – but more wins. He wanted to contend for championships so he joined the Golden State Warriors in 2013.

During that first season with the Warriors, he started every game like usual but the team didn't advance past the first round. During his second year with the Warriors, he was relegated to the bench for the first time in his career. After starting every game of his career for 10 straight years, Andre Iguodola would not hear his name called by the public address announcer prior to the game. But that didn't matter to him. Remember, he wanted more. He wanted to be a part of something bigger than himself.

A strange thing happened during the first year of Iguodola's career that he served in the role of reserve - The Golden State Warriors won the NBA Championship and he was named the 2015 NBA Finals MVP. His sacrifice paid off. In his first four years with the Warriors, his stats were at an all-time low as he only averaged 7.9 points per game and took only 6 shots per game but he earned two championship rings and the respect of an entire league.

In 2015, in a poll of all the NBA's general managers, they overwhelmingly selected him as the league's best role player. His role was no longer to be the leading scorer, but it was no less important. In his world, the goal of winning a championship or multiple championships was much more important than being an all-star or scoring points.

SCOTTIE PIPPEN

Scottie Pippen is in the Basketball Hall of Fame. He was also named as one of the NBA's Top-50 players of all-time, but to many people, the six-time NBA champion is still remembered for the time that he wasn't on the court. He is remembered for a moment in time when he was guilty of performing one of the Top-50 most unsportsmanlike acts of all time, according to the website *complex.com*.

The New York Knicks were leading Pippen's Chicago Bulls 2-0 in the 1994 Eastern Conference semifinals. Game Three was tied at 102 with just 1.8 seconds left in the game. This should have been Scottie Pippen's time to shine since Michael Jordan was no longer playing basketball as he was taking time away to take a swing at playing professional baseball. Pippen would average 22 points, 8.7 rebounds, 5.6 assists and 2.9 steals per game as he would finish that year as third in the MVP voting. But in this situation, coach Phil Jackson chose to have Pippen inbounds the ball and it would be Toni Kukoc, the new budding star, that would take the last shot. Pippen was furious and refused to go into the game. Phil Jackson had to call a second timeout once he realized that there were only four Chicago Bulls on the floor. Once play resumed, Kukoc hit the game winning fadeaway 22-foot shot at the buzzer.

It was rumored that Pippen resented or was jealous of "the Croatian Sensation", who ended up being named Second-Team All-Rookie that year. Regardless of his feelings for Kukoc, it was evident that Pippen was selfish and lost focus of the goal for at least one moment in one game. Basketball is a true team sport and it requires five players to play as one unit. There are five players and only one ball. The team goal must be more important than the role.

Pippen might have been one of the greatest but in this situation, it was determined that he could better serve the team as the inbounder. He might have been the team's best inbounder. The coach might have determined that nobody else could inbound the ball or make the proper decision as well as Pippen but that someone might have the ability to hit a shot. A coach's job is to make the best decision with the information available to them at that moment. A player's job is to buy into the concept of team and be willing to play the role to accomplish the team's goal.

MIRACLE ON ICE

One of the most dominating teams in the history of sports was the Soviet Union's hockey team. Coming into the 1980 Winter Olympics, they had won the gold medal in the four previous Olympic games. In a three-game series in 1979 against an NHL All-Star team that featured 20 future Hall of Famers, the Soviets won two of three including the final game 6-0. They also had their backup goalie in the net for that game.

It didn't appear that any team could defeat the Soviets, especially the Americans, who had the youngest team in the Olympics. In fact, less than two weeks prior to the 1980 Olympic games in Lake Placid, the two teams faced off in an exhibition game at the Madison Square Garden. The Soviets won 10-3 in a game that probably wasn't even that close. However, Coach Herb Brooks had a master plan of how to mold his individual players to become a team capable of beating the Soviet machine.

Brooks was once quoted as saying that he didn't want the best players, but that he wanted the right players. Not only was the team the youngest but it was made up of college players mainly from the University of Minnesota and Boston University. These two programs were extremely successful. They were also bitter rivals and hated one another – even having a big fight prior to their 1976 NCAA semifinal matchup.

Early on in the practice sessions, Coach Brooks would ask his players who they played for and the responses were always the same, "I'm so-and-so and I play at such-and-such college." This went on for many weeks. After one particular exhibition game in which they played terribly, Coach Brooks made them do sprints after the game. It was grueling and tempers were flaring. Eventually, captain Mike Eruzione would stand up and say "My name is Mike Eruzione…and I play for Team USA." That was what Coach Brooks wanted to hear. He ended the sprints and the players truly came together for the first time and skated off the ice as a team.

This group of guys that not only hated one another but were like everyone else in that they thought the Soviets were invincible eventually came together as one unit. They defeated the Soviets 4-3 in the semifinals and would go on to defeat Finland in the gold medal game. The "Miracle on Ice" was named the "Greatest Moment in Sports History" by Sports Illustrated.

Did someone on your team steal your girlfriend or boyfriend? Did someone say something mean to you? Does a certain team member annoy you? So what? The University of Minnesota and Boston University hockey players hated each other but eventually came together as teammates and pulled off the greatest upset in sports history. If they can do it, why can't you? When you come to practice, you are a team, not a collection of individuals. When it's game-time, your opponent is in the other colored jersey, not your teammates.

The 1000:1 underdog 1980 Olympic hockey team proved that it is possible to overcome any challenge and defeat any opponent if you come together as a team and completely buy into a common goal.

MIAMI DOLPHINS – NO NAME DEFENSE

The 1972 Miami Dolphins are the only team in NFL history to go undefeated for the entire season and win the Super Bowl in the same year. The 2007 New England Patriots also went undefeated in the regular season but they were not able to win the Super Bowl that year. The '72 Dolphins were led by a unit called the No-Name Defense. They could have been called the Team-First Defense, No-Ego Defense, or the Together Defense because they played as one unit and didn't care who got the credit as long as they were performing together and helping the Dolphins win.

Many of those players were not famous names on their own but they ended up getting recognized with awards because they played on a defense that got a lot of publicity. Each player became better and more famous because of the team that they played on, not the other way around. Without the chemistry and unselfish nature of those players, the Dolphins defense would not have been as good because they were better together than they were individually. By checking their egos at the door, that team made history and became, arguably, the greatest team of all-time.

CRYING IN THE LOCKER ROOM

My team was coming off a tough loss against a team that we were supposed to defeat. The next game was on the road against a team that was very talented and had beaten us the year before. We went into that game trying to bounce back from our upset loss two days earlier. Everything seemed to go right for us in the first half. Our defense was creating turnovers and it seemed like our basket was twice as big as we made an incredibly high percentage of shots. Halftime came and we were winning by 30 points! I always give the team about five minutes by themselves at halftime. After talking with my assistants and giving the team their normal five minutes, I went into the locker room. What I saw was completely unexpected.

We were up by 30 points on the road against a good team. Instead of smiles, there were plenty of concerned faces. In the corner was one of our starters crying. Shawna was surrounded by many of her teammates. Immediately I tried to find out what was wrong. Had she checked her cell phone and found out that a friend or relative had died? Was she sick? Did she have some personal problems going on? No, it wasn't any of that. Shawna was upset because she was playing badly and hadn't received as much playing time. She was embarrassed at how badly she had played. Remember, we are winning by 30 points against a good team. Not only was she not focused at the moment, but she had dragged a number of her teammates down with her.

Instead of celebrating the good things that we had done in the first half and confirming what was needed in the second half, we were spending our energies on a player that was only concerned about herself. Instead of wallowing in self-pity, she should have been high-fiving and applauding her teammates for playing so well. She could even have thanked them for having her back and picking up the slack since she didn't play her best.

Instead of reinforcing and reminding the team of our game plan for the second half, we spent the entire halftime dealing with a player that was focused only on herself. We still managed to win the game but we played terribly and allowed the other team to make it close toward the end. It is hard to maximize your team's potential and lift your teammates up when you are only focused on yourself.

MARION BASKETBALL

One of the best examples that I have seen of a team coming together when it mattered most was the 2016 Marion Giants boys basketball team. Marion has a long and storied tradition of success in the state of Indiana. "Hoosier Hysteria" is alive and well in the Marion community, as they have the world's 5th largest high school gym with a seating capacity of 7,500 and have won seven state titles. Marion is home to Naismith Basketball Hall of Famer Stretch Murphy and professional players Zach Randolph, Julius Mays, Scott Wood, Jay Edwards and James Blackmon, Jr. In 2011, James Blackmon, Sr. came back to his hometown to coach Marion after winning two State Championships at another school. Going into the 2015-16 season, hopes were high as the Giants had a talented group of players.

Unfortunately, these talented players were never seemed to jell during the regular season. Despite having plenty of college coaches attending each game, the Marion Giants lost 7 games during the regular season. After being one of the preseason favorites, they now found themselves on the outside of the top-10. In fact, they finished 3rd in their conference. It seemed that the players were all playing for themselves and worried about their individual statistics. They would drop their shoulders and pout when a teammate would shoot the ball. They would argue with one another during games – not just on the bench, but on the court, as well. They were more concerned about their roles than they were about achieving their stated goal of winning a state championship.

Going into the state tournament, Coach Blackmon met with his players and laid out what was at stake in the next few weeks. He helped them refocus on their goals. He helped show them that by playing team ball and by putting their selfish desires aside, that they actually would put themselves in a better position to get a college scholarship. The more they won and kept playing, the more impressive they would appear to college scouts. Additionally, the longer that they played in the tournament, the more exposure that they would get to college scouts that might be seeing them for the first time.

He reminded them that they had a chance to make history. If they won an 8th state championship, no team in Indiana would have more. This was an opportunity that they would look back upon with pride for the rest of their life. The Marion Giants, led by future Division I players Reggie Jones and Vijay Blackmon, played inspired, and most importantly, unselfish basketball for seven straight games and won a State Championship.

There are two main traits at the core of all losing teams – lack of ability and selfishness. The Marion Giants certainly were not lacking talent. When they played for themselves, they had a disappointing regular season. However, when they came together with a common goal, their talent was able to thrive and they were able to maximize their potential. They also added a new piece of jewelry to their collection as they earned a championship ring.

TONY ROMO/DAK PRESCOTT

Tony Romo became the Dallas Cowboys starting quarterback in 2006. In the next ten years, he would lead the Cowboys to the playoffs four times. In a franchise that has had some legendary quarterbacks, Romo would go on to set many team records, including most touchdown passes, most passing yards and most games of 300+ passing yards. In a 2016 preseason game, Romo would, unfortunately, break his collarbone. As a result of this freak injury, rookie Dak Prescott, a 4th round draft pick out of Mississippi State University, would take over the reins until Romo was ready to return.

Even though it appeared that Romo was healthy enough to return, he held a press conference on November 15, 2016. On November 15, 2016, the Cowboys had an 8-1 record with the rookie quarterback. However, there were some serious questions concerning the immediate future. Romo appeared to be healthy and he was, after all, one of the greatest quarterbacks in Cowboys history. A promising season might be torpedoed by a quarterback controversy.

But on this day, the four-time Pro Bowler, Tony Romo would call a press conference and provide one of the greatest examples of leadership. His sincere and unselfish words would be applauded. Two tweets by television sports personalities, in particular, were representative of the general sentiment regarding Romo's leadership example:

> Real leaders are those who lead when it's not about them. Tony Romo is exhibiting real leadership right now. (Trey Wingo, ESPN personality)

> Just watched Romo. Talk about impressive. How hard must that be for him? In 11 weeks, from irreplaceable guy to "carry the clipboard, pal." (Peter King from the MMQB)

Here is what Romo said at his press conference in its' entirety because it bears repeating. There are a lot of good lessons to learn from this speech:

> To say the first half of this season has been emotional would be a huge understatement. Getting hurt when you feel like you have the best team you've ever had is a soul-crushing moment for me. Then to learn it's not three to four weeks but 10 is another blow. And through it all, you have a tremendous amount of guilt on having let your teammates, fans, and organization down. After all, they were depending on you to bring them a championship.

> That's what quarterbacks are supposed to do. That's how we're judged. I love that. I still do. But then here you are, sidelined, without any real ability to help your teammates win on the field. That's when you're forced to come face to face with what's happening.

> Seasons are fleeting. Games become more precious. Chances for success diminish. Your potential successor has arrived. Injured two years in a row, and now in your mid-30s. The press is whispering, everyone has doubts, you spent

your career working to get here. Now we have to start all over.

You almost feel like an outsider. The coaches are sympathetic, but they still have to coach and you're not there. It's a dark place, probably the darkest it's ever been. You're sad and down and out and you ask yourself why did this have to happen. It's in this moment that you find out who you really are and what you're really about.

You see football is a meritocracy. You aren't handed anything. You earn everything, every single day, over and over again, you have to prove it. That's the way the NFL, that's the way football works.

A great example of this is Dak Prescott and what he's done. He's earned the right to be our quarterback. As hard as that is for me to say, he's earned that right. He's guided our team to an 8-1 record and that's hard to do. If you think for a second that I don't want to be out there, then you've probably never felt the pure ecstasy of competing and winning. That hasn't left me. In fact, it may burn more now than ever.

It's not always easy to watch. I think anybody who has been in this position understands that. But what is clear is that I was that kid once, stepping in having to prove yourself. I remember the feeling like it was yesterday. It really is an incredible time in your life.

And if I remember one thing from back then it's the people who helped me along when I was young, and if I can be that to Dak, you know, I've tried to be and I will be going forward.

I think you all know something magical is happening to our team. I'm not going to allow this situation to negatively affect Dak or this football team by becoming a constant distraction. I think Dak knows that I have his back and I think he knows that I have mine.

Ultimately, it's about the team. It's what we've preached our entire lives. I can remember when I was a kid just starting out and wanting to be part of something bigger than myself, for every high school kid out there or college player, there's greatness in being the kind of teammate who truly wants to be part of a team. Everyone wants to be the reason they're winning or losing. Every single one of us wants to be that person. But there are special moments that come from a shared commitment to play a role while doing it together.

That's what you remember. Not your stats or your prestige. But the relationships and the achievement that you created through a group. It's hard to do but there is great joy in that. And all the while your desire burns to be the best you've ever been. You can be both. I've figured that out in this process. It's what separates sports from everything else. It's why we love it. It's why we trust it. It's why I still want to play and compete.

Lastly, I just want to leave you with something I've learned in this process as well. I feel like we all have two battles, or two enemies going on, one with the man across from you, the second is with the man inside of you. I think once you control the one inside of you, the one across from you really doesn't matter. I think that's what we're all trying to do.

Thank you guys. Appreciate it.

If this speech doesn't make you appreciate and respect a guy, then I am not sure anything would. Romo was capable of playing but chose the high road. He made a difficult decision that was not in his best interest but it was what the team needed. You are either being a positive or negative leader. There is no staying neutral. Romo's situation was a classic example of this. He could have stayed quiet and let the media firestorm continue, which would only put more undue pressure on Dak Prescott or he could choose to do something about it.

With the best offensive line in the NFL, the NFL's leading rusher at running back and plenty of weapons to throw to, there is little doubt that Tony Romo would have led the Cowboys to a great season. But it would be Prescott who would end up having the magical season and leading the Cowboys to a 13-3 record. Along the way, he would break Tom Brady's record for most consecutive pass attempts without an interception to start a career. Prescott would also be named the NFL Offensive Rookie of the Year.

We can only speculate what would have happened if Tony Romo had not supported Prescott. However, we can probably accurately guess that it would have made everyone's job harder and taken the focus off of the goal of winning. Romo understood that the role is more important than the goal.

KENTUCKY BASKETBALL

During the 2012 season, the Kentucky Wildcats had two extremely talented players that would end up going #1 and #2 in the upcoming NBA draft. Essentially, UK had the two best players according to the NBA. Anthony Davis and Michael Kidd-Gilchrist were considered the two best professional basketball prospects – and they were on the same team. There was a lot of talent. A lot of mouths to feed. Surely, Davis and Kidd-Gilchrist would lead the way since they were the clear-cut best players on the team, right? They did lead the way, but not in the way that you would think.

They led by putting the team-first, not their individual goals. Davis ended up being fourth on the Wildcats in field-goal attempts. Kidd-Gilchrist was fifth on the team in field-goal attempts. On most teams, that wouldn't fly. On most teams with this much talent, players would be bickering about playing time and shot distribution, but not these guys. The two top NBA prospects were 4th and 5th on their team in shots. They didn't want shots, they wanted ships … championships. By buying into the team concept and sacrificing individual goals, they helped Kentucky win a national championship. In doing so, they also demonstrated that they weren't just talented but that they were winners.

CHANNING FRYE

Here's a question to consider. Let's say that you are a talented basketball player. You are not starting but you in the regular rotation, averaging nearly 9 points per game. During the playoffs, you make 7 of 9 three-pointers in a key game to propel your team to the next round. However, during the first four games of the seven-game Championship series, you only play a TOTAL of 33 minutes and your team lost three of those four games. Not only have you not been playing much in those first four games, but your coach decides to bench you for the remaining three games. Remember, you were a big part of helping them get to the Championship series.

How would you react? Would you be happy? Where would your focus be? The general idea of this hypothetical situation is played out often across the country every day. An important player is benched. How does that player react? Does that player then sabotage the team or does that player provide the encouragement and support needed?

The situation described above is an actual situation that occurred during the 2016 NBA playoffs to Channing Frye, a 6'11" former 1st round draft pick and 10-year NBA veteran. Reflecting on the 2016 season with the Cleveland Cavs, Frye summarized his thoughts in *The Player's Tribune,*

> As we approached the Finals, we were cutting down the rotations; we wanted to stick to who we were defensively, and that involved going with more physical lineups against the Warriors. I knew there were going to be less opportunities for me, but I was cool. I'd be watching from the front row with my brothers.
>
> I think that closeness showed up in Game 7, which was the greatest game I've ever watched in my life. I was like, You know what? I gotta go to the back. I understood my role: Be a good teammate, stay ready for anything and support your bros.
>
> That game was epic.
>
> We just never gave up on each other, even when we got down momentarily. It was like, think about everything

you've done all summer, all year — your whole life, my whole life. We deserve this!

I was so into the game that when Steph Curry missed at the end and Mo Speights got the ball — and LeBron put his arms up — I was screaming, "Contest the shot!" And someone said, "We're up four." And I realized, Holy shit, we're going to win!

When the clock hit zero, I looked around and thought, Who am I supposed to hug? I hugged my friend Bret Brielmaier, I hugged Richard. I was hugging everyone I could find, the owners' wives, everybody. The magnitude of what we did didn't hit me till days later, and I lost it.

TTY

This summer, I taught her (Margaux, his daughter) and my son, Hendrix, "What do we call Daddy now?"

They say, "Champion."

Channing Frye couldn't have been happy to be benched. If it wasn't for Frye, Cleveland may not have even been in the Finals. Players want to play, but Frye wanted to be more than a player. He wanted to be a champion and that would take more than demonstrating his talents on the court. It took him demonstrating his leadership talents on the bench and in the locker room. His positive attitude and ability to put the goal above his desired role made him a champion.

BE A STAR IN YOUR ROLE

The Cleveland Cavaliers won the 2016 NBA Championship after they came back from a seemingly insurmountable 3-1 deficit against the Golden State Warriors. The Warriors had the home-court advantage after winning the most regular season games in NBA history. The Cavs were led by Lebron James but they needed more than a superstar to win the series. Winning three in a row to close out the series was unprecedented but the Cavs did it, not just because of a superstar but because of another kind of star. All year Tristan Thompson remained in the shadow of his superstar teammates,

James, Kevin Love, and Kyrie Irving, doing the dirty work. The NBA finals were no exception, rather just with more at stake, and he responded. Here is how Michael Singer of *USA Today* described his Game-6 performance,

> ' He didn't overwhelm the Golden State Warriors like LeBron James did, and he didn't confound their defense like Kyrie Irving did, but Cleveland Cavaliers forward Tristan Thompson played his role, and he played it to perfection in the Cavs' Game 6 rout.

> …Thompson's value is in the dirty work. He's not the type to post 41 points like James, and he'll never engender the defensive attention of a ball-handler like Irving. But it's his consistent effort that his teammates have learned to rely on.

> …The Cavs forced a Game 7 with their 115-101 victory over the Warriors, and Thompson, behind 15 points and 16 rebounds, had a team-high plus-32 in plus-minus.

In the press conference after that Game 6 performance, Tristan Thompson talked about his mentality,

> "Like LeBron and Kyrie said, be a star in your role. Be a star in your role, and for me, that's high energy, use my motor,
> . just play hard. Play hard, be relentless, and that's what I bring to this team. That's my job, just be a star in your role."

Tristan Thompson's huge double-double in Game 6 of the 2016 NBA Finals and unselfish play in all of the games helped lead the Cleveland Cavs to the World Championship. Good thing for Cavs fans and players that he didn't pout about his boring and un-glamorous role. He might not have been a star but he was a star in his role. He might not be Lebron James, but he will always be able to call himself a CHAMPION!

10.
OUTWORK YOUR TALENT

"God gives gifts to everyone but that means nothing. It's what you make of them that counts."
– Ronaldinho

""If you're struggling with your shooting, then do other things on the basketball court. Get steals, get assists, get rebounds – do anything on the court to help the team win."
– Allen Iverson

"If I'm not doing it right, I want coach to tell me so I can fix it."
– Steph Curry

"Talent is never enough. With few exceptions, the best players are the hardest workers."
– Magic Johnson

""Some people want it to happen, some people wish it would happen, successful people make it happen."
– Michael Jordan

Have you ever thought that you were good enough? Do you ever feel that you have arrived as a player? Do you get frustrated when your coach expects more out of you? Have you ever wondered why teammates or coaches might push you a little harder? Do you think that being on your game or working hard most of the time is acceptable?

Are you okay with having 99% effort? Did you know that if pilots were successful 99% of the time that there would be 24 plane crashes per day? If hospitals were correct 99% of the time when matching up a baby with its' correct parents that roughly 11 babies would be given to the wrong parents each day?

Every day we are faced with the choice of whether we will maximize our talents and potential. Some of us have more talent in certain areas than others. It doesn't matter if you are a third-string player or an all-conference performer, you can still underachieve or overachieve. You can continually decide if you will maximize your talent. Your talent is a starting point. It gives an athlete an opportunity but what you do with it determines the level of success that you and your team experience.

You and your team probably have morning workouts, team film sessions & practice. But guess what? So, does every other team. What are you doing to be different? Every baseball team in America has a leading hitter, a leading fielder and sends out 9 starters for a game. How will you and your team differentiate itself from the competition? How will you outperform yourself and what you think you are capable of? Talent is God-given; Excellence is a choice.

BOSTON RED SOX

Sports Illustrated said that the Boston Red Sox 2004 season was "the Most Amazing Season in History" as they awarded the entire team its' prestigious Sportsmen of the Year honor. All the Red Sox did that year was win the team's first World Series Championship in 86 years. For Boston fans and the Red Sox that was a long drought. The Red Sox won the first ever World Series in 1903 and then won four more before Babe Ruth was traded from Boston to the New York Yankees prior to the 1919 season. Many believed that the "curse of the Bambino" was real since they didn't win another World Series after that … until 2004.

Not only did the 2004 Red Sox win but they made history doing it.

In the American League Conference Series, they lost the first three games to their arch-enemy Yankees. In the fourth game, they trailed in the ninth inning. Losing this game would mean a New York sweep as they would then advance to another World Series appearance.

However, there was no quit in this Boston team as they rallied in the ninth inning to win. They then proceeded to win the next three games to complete the greatest series comeback in baseball history. No team had ever been down 3-0 in a series and came back to win. The Red Sox would then complete the magical season by defeating the St. Louis Cardinals in the World Series. How did they do this after 86 years? What was the secret? To listen to the players, it was all about chemistry and camaraderie.

In Joe McDonald's *ESPN.com* article celebrating the 2004 team, outfielder Kevin Millar provided a number of insights that gave a look into the mindset and mentality of a group of individuals that truly came together as a team,

> "The group of guys, the family, it wasn't just a team. It was a unit that literally hung out together and ate together and liked each other. You can't buy that. You remember the tightness of that team. It wasn't the best players. We had a few superstars in Pedro and Manny, but we were the best unit if that makes sense.
>
> You hear a lot, 'What's chemistry? If you don't have the players, you don't have chemistry.' Bull. You've got to pull for each other because you're not fooling us. You can't fool your teammates. If you feel that someone is pulling against Keith Foulke because he wants to be the closer and doesn't know his role, you feel that. If you're pulling against Pedro Martinez because he wants to be the guy, you feel that. We pulled for each other and that's what was cool."

In the same article, closer Keith Foulke talked about the responsibility that they had to one another,

> "We were buddies and when Johnny [Damon] is out there

running into walls, that makes you want to work harder to make sure that effort doesn't go for naught. We're a family and you go to battle with your brothers."

Sure, they had some talented players but they only finished 3ʳᵈ in the American League regular season that year. They were surely not as talented overall as the Yankees or probably even the Cardinals but they had the intangibles. As manager Terry Francona said,

"We have a lot of characters that have a lot of character."

Chemistry, camaraderie and high character players were the ingredients that allowed them to persevere and overcome all obstacles to win a World Championship. Those are ingredients that any team in any sport can have if they want them. They are also necessary if you are going to succeed in the face of adversity.

IT'S ONLY ONE POSSESSION

Every possession matters. Every minute matters. Every day matters. What we do in practice today will help or hurt us in our next game. Everything matters. In a close win or loss, most people remember the official's call or the key free throw toward the end of the game. Though not as memorable, are the turnover or shot with 2:00 to go in the 3rd quarter that counted just as much. Below is basketball poem by Jeff Smith that highlights this philosophy of making every moment matter…

It was only one possession,
Why must my coach scream?
My poor defense permitted the basket
But what can one hoop mean?

As the pass comes my direction,
And I fumble it into the stands,
The coach's' voice rings loud and clear,
"Catch with your eyes and hands!"

C'mon coach, it's a single possession,
Our team will be okay.
It's just the first two minutes,
My gosh, we've got all day.

At the ten-minute mark I remember,
That the center is strong and stout.
A put back for two, quite simply is due
To my failure to turn and block out.

But it was only one possession,
I didn't commit a crime,
My team is still ahead and I'm playing well,
And there's still plenty of time.

As the halftime buzzer is sounding,
And I watch the ball bank in,
I know I will hear from my loving coach
Of my questionable effort to defend.

But it was only one possession
Coach-don't have a heart attack!
We're down by one, but we're having fun,
I know we'll get the lead back!

The second half mirrors the first,
But it's early; it's not a big deal,
That's my failure to use a bounce fake,
Results in an unlikely steal.

But quickly I sink a jumper,
I'm greeted by high fives and slaps,
But the next possession I give up a lay-up
While suffering a metal lapse.

But it's only one possession,
C'mon Coach, "Chill Out."

It's crazy to see you disgusted
As you slap the assistant and shout.

"Victory favors the team making fewest mistakes.
Single possessions are the key.
So treat them like gold and do as your told,
And play with intensity.

I step on the line for one and one,
But I'm having a concentration lapse.
The ball soars through the air, Good Lord, it's a brick!
I'm afraid the support will collapse.

In post-game I sit at my locker,
Pondering what more could I do.
I realize the value of each possession,
What a shame that we lost by two.

Most players can relate to this poem. In the course of a long game, it doesn't seem that one little play here or there matters. However, it matters a great deal to the player that ends up losing a game by one point. If you think small things don't matter, think of the last game you lost by one point. "Should of", "could of", "would of" are all tough phrases to swallow when you have lost a close game. But you can't just show up for a game and decide that you are going to do all of the little things right.

You do the little things right because you have developed the daily habits that lead you to be automatic. When you don't even have to think about boxing-out, diving for a loose ball or helping a teammate up off of the ground then you have developed positive habits. The ancient philosopher Aristotle said that we are what we repeatedly do. Excellence is not an act, but a habit. Do you want to be excellent at your sport? Do you want to be respected and liked? Do you want to be a champion? You are what you repeatedly do. You are what your habits say you are.

WAYNE GRETZKY

Wayne Gretzky was the such a great hockey player that he earned the nickname "The Great One." For further proof of his greatness, he is far and away the NHL's all-time leading scorer. In fact, he accumulated more assists in his career than any other player has with assists and goals combined! Here is a story Stu Hackel that he did for SI.com where Gretzky talks about the 1982-1983 season when they lost to the New York Islanders in the Stanley Cup finals. This was the moment when he truly understood what it meant to win and not just be talented,

> Wayne Gretzky learned about that price in 1983 when he and his young Oilers teammates lost in their first Cup final to the Islanders, who had won four straight championships. Walking by the Islanders' dressing room after the last game, Gretzky and teammate Kevin Lowe were surprised to see the Isles not whooping it up.

> "Trottier was icing what looked like a painful knee," he wrote in his autobiography. "Potvin was getting stuff rubbed on his shoulder. Guys were limping around with black eyes and bloody mouths. It looked more like a morgue in there than a champion's locker room. And here we were perfectly fine and healthy.

> "That's why they won and we lost. They took more punishment than we did. They dove into more boards, stuck their faces in front of more pucks, threw their bodies into more pileups. They sacrificed everything they had.

> "And that's when Kevin said something I'll never forget. He said, 'That's how you win championships.'"

Gretzky and his Edmonton Oilers proceeded to win five of the next seven Stanley Cup Championships after this loss in 1982-1983. "The Great One" and his teammates learned how to outwork their talent. They found ways to be more than just a collection of talented individuals. Are you talented? What are you doing to outwork your talent and be more than the skills and abilities that you possess? Sometimes the intangibles are what separates champions from contenders.

PEYTON MANNING

Peyton Manning played the quarterback position as well as anyone in the history of the NFL for 18 years. He played 14 of those with the Indianapolis Colts and was the MVP of Super Bowl 41 in 2006. The Colts eventually released him after having neck surgery and missing the entire 2011 season. He then went on to play four seasons with the Denver Broncos. Manning would quarterback the team to the Super Bowl 50 championship in his final season.

He holds many NFL records including most touchdown passes and passing yards. His five league MVP's are the most in NFL history. He is also the only quarterback to ever start four Super Bowls with a different head coach each time. Manning is arguably the greatest passer in league history. Even though he was immensely talented, he developed the habit of outworking his talent. He didn't just rely on his physical skills. He understood that talent didn't equal good and that good was the enemy of great. He always kept working – not only on his physical skills but his mental skills as well.

Former UCLA All-American and NFL defensive back Rahim Moore once made a comment to Ben Hochman of the *Denver Post* regarding Manning's mentality and work ethic, which was followed up by a Manning rebuttal,

> "We know when he gets on the field, he's going hard — like as if he never had a penny. That's how hard he works. You would think he never had done a commercial, none of that. He's training like he's a free agent."

> Let it sink in. What a quote, right? Peyton Manning, one of the best talents of his generation, attacks practice as if his career is on the line.

> "I had a coach taught me at an early age of treating practice like a game," Manning said of <u>David Cutcliffe</u>, his beloved coach from his Tennessee days. "To me, this is where you become a better football team out here on the practice field. You don't just show up on a game and expect to be a good football team. I appreciate those words [from] Rahim. I

think somebody taught me to practice like that at a young age. That would be my advice to any young players. To me, this is where you become a better football team, out here on the practice field. You don't just show up on a game and expect to be a good football team."

It is nearly impossible to find someone that says something negative about Peyton Manning. That is because he was so respected – not just because of his talent, but because of his character and leadership. He was so successful because he had a high level mix of talent and intangibles. He was the most prepared player on the team. He was universally regarded as his team's hardest worker. When you are the team's star and provide the example for these intangibles, then it is going to be hard for teammates to be lazy.

It is not surprising that his teams appeared in four Super Bowls during his career and that he ended up winning nearly 69% of the games that he started. Only Tom Brady has won more games than Peyton Manning's 200 regular-season wins. Other talented quarterbacks have played in the NFL but Manning's work ethic and preparation have differentiated him from them. How about you? Are you outworking your talent or just relying on your talent? What are the extra things that you are doing to take you and your team to a higher level?

WHAT IT TAKES TO BE #1

In 1960 the Green Bay Packers were leading the Philadelphia Eagles 13-10 in the fourth quarter of the NFL Championship game. With about five minutes to go, the Eagles scored and hung on to win 17-13. The Packers and their legendary coach Vince Lombardi were devastated. When the summer came and the team met to go through training camp, Lombardi had a different approach to football. He was going to stress fundamentals more than ever. He was going to emphasize winning habits more than ever. David Maraniss told it this way in his book, *When Pride Still Mattered: A Life Of Vince Lombardi*,

> He took nothing for granted. He began a tradition of starting from scratch, assuming that the players were blank slates who carried over no knowledge from the year

before… He began with the most elemental statement of all. "Gentlemen," he said, holding a pigskin in his right hand, "this is a football."

Lombardi became obsessed with teaching fundamentals and establishing positive daily habits in his players. He would constantly reinforce the proper ways to tackle and block. It was similar to when basketball coach John Wooden would teach his players the correct way to put on their socks and tie their shoes. Another Hall of Fame football coach Chuck Noll of the Pittsburgh Steelers used to say, "Champions are champions not because they do anything extraordinary, but because they do the ordinary things better than anyone else."

That loss in the 1960 game would end up being the only playoff loss that legendary football coach Vince Lombardi would suffer in his career. In fact, six months after the training camp that started the re-emphasis on fundamentals, the Packers won the NFL Championship 37-0 by defeating the New York Giants. The Super Bowl Championship trophy would eventually be named the Lombardi trophy.

Coach Lombardi was also famous for a quote about winning and habits that are worth repeating,

> "Winning is not a sometime thing; it's an all the time thing. You don't win once in a while; you don't do things right once in a while; you do them right all the time. Winning is a habit. Unfortunately, so is losing.

> "There is no room for second place. There is only one place in my game, and that's first place. I have finished second twice in my time at Green Bay, and I don't ever want to finish second again. There is a second place bowl game, but it is a game for losers played by losers. It is and always has been an American zeal to be first in anything we do, and to win, and to win, and to win.

> "Every time a football player goes to play his trade he's got to play from the ground up - from the soles of his feet right up to his head. Every inch of him has to play. Some guys

play with their heads. That's O.K. You've got to be smart to be number one in any business. But more importantly, you've got to play with your heart, with every fiber of your body. If you're lucky enough to find a guy with a lot of head and a lot of heart, he's never going to come off the field second.

"Running a football team is no different than running any other kind of organization - an army, a political party or a business. The principles are the same. The object is to win - to beat the other guy. Maybe that sounds hard or cruel. I don't think it is.

"It is a reality of life that men are competitive and the most competitive games draw the most competitive men. That's why they are there - to compete. To know the rules and objectives when they get in the game. The object is to win fairly, squarely, by the rules - but to win.

"And in truth, I've never known a man worth his salt who in the long run, deep down in his heart, didn't appreciate the grind, the discipline. There is something in good men that really yearns for discipline and the harsh reality of head to head combat.

"I don't say these things because I believe in the 'brute' nature of man or that men must be brutalized to be combative. I believe in God, and I believe in human decency. But I firmly believe that any man's finest hour - his greatest fulfillment to all he holds dear - is that moment when he has to work his heart out for a good cause and he's exhausted on the field of battle - victorious."

What kind of habits do you have? Do you have winning habits? The former University of Oregon and NFL head coach Chip Kelly had a motto that said, "Win the Day". Do you try to win every day?

Kelly would talk about doing the little things throughout each day that leads to victory – victory for that day, which would lead to victory for the week, which would lead to victory for the month, and so on. Your next win began a long time ago with daily victories and habits being developed.

Every major victory has countless minor victories along the way that made it possible. Very few teams go undefeated. You can't expect to win every day but you can win today. Tackle your goals in small increments. Win the little battles and you'll eventually win the war. Win enough days and you'll eventually be a winner. Winning is a habit. Unfortunately, so is losing.

UNLIKELY NBA CHAMPIONS

One of the greatest upsets in NBA playoff history was when the Dallas Mavericks defeated the Miami Heat to win the 2011 NBA Championship. Coming into that season, the Mavs had gotten bounced in the first-round in three of the previous four seasons. After beating the Trailblazers in the first round of the 2010-11 playoffs, they were then underdogs to the Los Angeles Lakers who were going for a four-peat.

They caught fire and swept Kobe Bryant and the Lakers. They then bested the Russell Westbrook/Kevin Durant-led Oklahoma City Thunder. Even after pulling off two straight upsets in the Western Conference Playoffs, very few people gave them a chance as they went up against the Miami Heat super team that had been put together the previous summer with Lebron James, Chris Bosh, and Dwayne Wade. The Big Three, who had only lost three games in the entire playoffs up to the Finals, ended up succumbing to Dirk Nowitzki and the Mavs.

Nowitzki was the unquestioned star of the Mavericks but he was getting older. The core group of players that was his supporting cast was also aging veterans that had never won an NBA Championship, such as Jason Kidd, Shawn Marion, Jason Terry and Tyson Chandler. According to Neil Paine of the website *FiveThirtyEight.com*, Dirk Nowitzki's supporting cast with the Mavs was the fifth-worst in NBA Finals history since 1985.

Do you want to know why a group of less-talented players beat the Big Three? One of the answers was revealed years later. At the end of the 2016-17 season, a vote was taken among NBA players. Dirk Nowitzki won the 2016-17 NBA Teammate of the Year award. However, what was just as revealing was that Tyson Chandler finished second and Jason Terry finished fourth in the player voting. Jason Kidd just finished up his third year coaching the Milwaukee Bucks. Milwaukee had the 2016-17 Rookie of the Year in Malcolm Brogdon and the league's Most Improved Player in Giannis Antetokounmpo.

You want to know why an underdog team shocked the NBA, it was because they had a bunch of guys that were good teammates and had the proper focus. They were united by a common goal. Is your team just a collection of talented individuals? Are you being the best teammate that you can be? Are you influencing your teammates to stay focused and to be the best that they can be? If you want to maximize your team's potential then you need to increase the impact of each teammate. Want a better team? Have better teammates.

LARRY BIRD

Larry Bird is one of the greatest basketball players ever and was on the original Dream Team that dominated in the 1992 Olympics. The "Hick from French Lick" led little known Indiana State to the 1979 NCAA Championship Game while being named the Naismith College Player of the Year. He then went on to play his entire NBA career for the Boston Celtics, where he won three world championships. The 6'9" forward's career averages were 24.3 ppg, 10.0 rpg, and 6.3 apg. In 1998 he was inducted into the Naismith Basketball Hall of Fame.

He was considered one of the hardest workers and fiercest competitors. In Mark Shaw's book, *Larry Legend*, Bird's desire to outwork his talent was highlighted with this example, in which he was doing things that other players didn't do regularly,

> "While most players waltzed into the locker room the required 90 minutes before game time, Bird has been on the floor by at least 6:00, more than two hours before tip-off. In the loneliness of Boston Garden, with only attendants and a few Celtics season ticket holders present, Bird shot more than 300 practice shots. He'd start with 6 to 10 free throws, move out on the court a bit, and then start firing away at a comfortable pace as comrade Joe Qatato hit him with perfect passes. Then the 'Parquet Picasso,' as he was dubbed, would speed up the routine and by the end of the workout throw up rapid-fire shots, many featuring the Bird

drop back a step maneuver that guaranteed him an opening from every angle."

Even though Bird had a knack for scoring and was a prolific shooter, he was always trying to get better. In Bird's autobiography, *Drive*, he said,

"As a kid, I always thought I was behind and I needed that extra hour to catch up. A coach once told me, "No matter how many shots you take, somewhere there's a kid out there taking one more. If you dribble a million times a day, someone is dribbling a million and one."

Whenever I'd get ready to call it a day, I'd think, "No. Somebody else is still practicing. Somebody-somewhere-is playing that extra ten or fifteen minutes and he's going to beat me someday."

I'd practice some more and then I'd think, "Maybe that guy is practicing his free throws now." So I'd go to the line and practice my free throws and that would take another hour.

I don't know if I practiced more than anybody, but I sure practiced enough. I still wonder if somebody-somewhere-was practicing more than me."

Bird's words sound strikingly similar to what Lebron James said about Kobe Bryant in a Mark Lamport-Stokes article for Reuters,

"I knew I had to be better because of Kobe Bryant. I knew he was in the gym and I knew he was working on his game. And I knew he was great. So every day that I didn't want to work out or every day I felt like I couldn't give more, I always thought of Kobe. Because I knew that he was getting better."

If you are bad, you can be average. If you are average, you can strive for good. Finally, if you are doing little things, leading yourself and outworking your talent, you can go from good-to-great.

STEPH CURRY

During Steph Curry's sophomore season in college, he averaged 25.9 PPG and led Davidson to the NCAA Tournament. During the tournament, they earned three straight upsets against Gonzaga, Georgetown, and Wisconsin. They would lose in the Elite Eight to the eventual champion Kansas Jayhawks by two. He was second-team All-American scoring guard and perhaps the best shooter in the nation but that wouldn't be enough for the next level.

Instead of leaving early he decided to come back to Davidson for one more year so that he could play point guard and maximize his potential in the NBA. During his junior year, he improved his assist total from 2.9 APG to 5.6 APG. That extra year proved valuable as it speeded up his transition to the NBA. He went on to become the NBA's first unanimous Most Valuable Player when he won the award in 2016 – as a point guard! He listened to key people and was coachable. This allowed him to reach his potential and help his team win the NBA Championship.

Talent is only a starting point. If you want to be truly great, then you must transcend your talent and learn how to do more. The best players are never satisfied. They have never arrived. Steph is a great example of someone that had talent that has squeezed everything he can out of it and more. He constantly wants to improve.

11.
QUICK LISTS

"A leader can't make excuses. There has to be quality in everything you do. Off the court, on the court, in the classroom."
– Michael Jordan

"Talent is important. But the single most important ingredient after you get the talent is internal leadership. It's not the coaches as much as one single person or people on the team who set higher standards than that team would normally set for itself. I really believe that that's been ultimately important for us."
– Mike Krzyzewski

Here are a number of quick hitters or lists that can generate thoughts about your leadership or that of your team. These are explored in further details in the free online resources that you have access to with your book purchase.

BOOST THE CONFIDENCE OF YOUR TEAMMATES
1. Clarify expectations
2. Celebrate successes
3. Point out the progress made
4. Promote their strengths
5. Help them with their weaknesses
6. Remember past successes
7. Praise them to others
8. Praise the in public
9. Work with them extra before or after practice
10. Applaud their work ethic

DUTIES OF A TEAM CAPTAIN

1. Put out locker room fires
2. Enforce & remind players of team standards and rules
3. Plan and organize off-court team activities
4. Lead form running, warmups and drills
5. Pay attention to what is going on and talking with team members
6. Determine tone in the locker room
7. Provide input to coaches and keeping them informed
8. Serve as public representative of the team
9. Set the tone for the team during practice
10. Trusted liaison between coach and team.

"NEXT PLAY" STRATEGIES

1. Stay focused on your goals
2. Remember your game plan
3. Visualize likely scenarios (and the appropriate responses) before practice and games
4. Stay positive
5. Become an active observer while on the bench. Stay mentally engaged thinking of what you would do in each situation
6. Trust the process rather than being consumed with results
7. Stay in the present. Make the best play that is possible now
8. Realize that you can only control what you can control
9. Verbally remind teammates "next play"

THINGS THAT EVERY PLAYER CAN DO

1. Be coachable
2. Be on time
3. Demonstrate a positive attitude
4. Do extra
5. Encourage teammates
6. Help others
7. Prepare
8. Provide energy
9. Put forth effort
10. Spread enthusiasm

HOW TO COMMUNICATE BETTER

1. Actually, listen instead of just waiting for your turn to speak.
2. Look them in the eye when they are talking to you – that means putting the phone down
3. Don't assume that they know what you meant or what you are thinking.
4. Pay attention to your body language because it oftentimes speaks so loudly that the other person can't hear the words coming out of your mouth.
5. Remember that everyone has a different personality even if they are your friends and you have similar interests.
6. Be open and honest with one another – but, also tactful and respectful. Sometimes there is a more appropriate time and place for certain honest communication
7. The old adage of "if you can't say anything nice then don't say anything" is not true. If you can't say anything nice, take a moment and find something nice to say. You might not like someone but you can always encourage in a positive way.
8. Don't interrupt them or try to defend yourself.
9. Try to see things from their perspective.
10. Avoid using too many absolutes.

THINGS THAT WILL DIFFERENTIATE YOUR LEADERSHIP

1. Learn from the past.
2. Learn to listen and listen to learn.
3. Be early, stay late and do a little bit extra.
4. Be an active observer. Learn from what you see happening. You don't have to make all of your own mistakes.
5. Turn your social media into a positive, motivating and encouraging platform.
6. Sit with different people at team meals. Be the person that everyone gets along with.
7. Sweep the floor or help set up cones before practice.
8. Get involved in community service
9. Put out fires on the team before they become fully engulfed.
10. Go over plays with your teammates.

WAYS TO DEMONSTRATE RESPECT

1. Maintain eye contact when others are talking (this means putting the phone down).
2. Pay attention to all of the instructions that are being given.
3. Pick up after yourself and others (leave the locker room cleaner than you found it).
4. Don't argue with an official even if they make a bad call.
5. Pick a player up when they've fallen down.
6. Say 'please' and 'thank you'.
7. Hold the door open for others.
8. Sit in the front couple of rows of classes and then pay attention.
9. Let others speak and actually listen to them.
10. Send thank you notes (they will be more memorable and will impress people).
11. Be on time.
12. Don't be sarcastic or embarrass others.
13. Take care of your body and health.
14. Avoid making people uncomfortable or putting people in compromising positions.
15. Keep an open mind about people's differences and their opinions.

10 MISTAKES CAPTAINS MAKE
(Craig Hillier)

1. Thinking the job is over after being elected or selected.
2. Trying to please everyone.
3. Not confronting difficult issues with the team.
4. Not confronting a difficult issue with a coach.
5. Not connecting with parents of teammates or players.
6. "Dissing" players or coaches behind their backs.
7. Not planning ahead.
8. Believing the only place leadership is shown revolves around a given sport.
9. Giving 80% effort and expecting 100% results.
10. Expecting to do a good job without leadership training.

TEAM ACTIVITIES THAT HELP OTHERS

1. Donate shoes that you don't use anymore.
2. Reading to or tutoring elementary kids.
3. Visiting nursing homes or hospitals (especially the children's wing).
4. Greet military personnel at airports when they return home. Maybe even give them some gifts.
5. Special appreciation days where you bake cookies or do something special for teachers, fire fighters, police officers, custodians, etc...
6. Serve people in the cafeteria by putting their trays away or getting them drink refills.
7. Hand out popsicles or bottled water at soccer games when it is hot. For cold games, you could pass out free hot cocoa.
8. Rake leaves or shovel snow for the elderly.
9. Rally around a cause (cancer, angel tree, toys for tots, adoption, poverty, water, etc...) and make that your project for the year (raising money and awareness).
10. Conduct a free sports clinic for kids in the area.
11. Ring bells for the Salvation Army during the Christmas season. You could wear your travel suits and pass out game schedules or camp brochures.
12. Volunteer to clean up trash at a community event or adopt a stretch of highway to clean up.
13. Paint, do lawn care or light maintenance work at a local YMCA or Boys & Girls Club.
14. Organize an Easter egg hunt for community kids.
15. Coach or host a special Olympics event.

7 HABITS OF HIGHLY EFFECTIVE PEOPLE
(Stephen Covey)

1. Be proactive
2. Begin with the end in mind
3. Put first things first
4. Think win-win
5. Seek first to understand, then to be understood
6. Synergize
7. Sharpen the saw

HOW TO TELL A CHAMP FROM A CHUMP

1. A champ says, "Let's find out;" a chump says, "Nobody knows."
2. When a champ makes a mistake, he says, "I was wrong;" when a chump makes a mistake, he says, "It wasn't my fault."
3. A champ knows how and when to say "Yes" and "No"; a chump says, "Yes, but" and "Perhaps not" at the wrong times, for the wrong reasons.
4. A champ isn't nearly as afraid of losing as a chump is secretly afraid of winning.
5. A champ works harder than a chump, and has more time; a chump is always "too busy" to do what is necessary.
6. A champ goes through a problem; a chump goes around it, and never gets past it.
7. A champ makes commitments, a chump makes promises.
8. A champ shows he's sorry by making up for it; a chump says "I'm sorry," but does the same thing the next time.
9. A champ knows what to fight for and what to compromise on; a chump compromises on what he shouldn't and fights for what isn't worth fighting about.
10. A champ says, "I'm good but not as good as I ought to be;" a chump says, "I'm not as bad as a lot of other people."
11. A champ listens; a chump just waits until it's his turn to talk.
12. A champ would rather be admired than liked, although he would prefer both; a chump would rather be liked than admired and is even willing to pay the price of mild contempt for it.
13. A champ respects those who are superior to him, and tries to learn something from them; a chump resents those who are superior to him and tries to find chinks in their armor.
14. A champ says, "There ought to be a better way to do it"; a chump says, "That's the way it's always been done here."
15. A champ says, "I'll do what it takes"; a chump says, "I can't."

WAYS PLAYERS SABOTAGE THEMSELVES OR THEIR TEAM

1. Let their teammates fail on or off the court.
2. Rely on others to lead instead of stepping up to the plate.
3. Don't do anything at all because they don't know where to start or the task seems insurmountable.
4. Stuck on their way of doing something and aren't open to a different perspective.
5. Forget about the big picture or their purpose.
6. Fail to honestly and accurately evaluate themselves.
7. Compartmentalize leadership roles.
8. Have a wrong idea about leadership.
9. Give up too quickly and not persevering through adversity.
10. Play the blame game or finding excuses.
11. Dwell on the past
12. Live in the past
13. Think that they have "arrived"
14. Roll their eyes or displaying bad body language
15. Focus entirely on results and not the process

13 RULES OF LEADERSHIP
(Colin Powell)

1. It ain't as bad as you think. It will look better in the morning.
2. Get mad, then get over it.
3. Avoid having your ego so close to your position that when your position falls, your ego goes with it.
4. It can be done!
5. Be careful what you choose. You may get it.
6. Don't let adverse facts stand in the way of a good decision.
7. You can't make someone else's choices. You shouldn't let someone else make yours.
8. Check small things.
9. Share credit.
10. Remain calm. Be kind.
11. Have a vision. Be demanding.
12. Don't take counsel of your fears or naysayers.
13. Perpetual optimism is a force multiplier.

9 WAYS TO BE A GREAT TEAM MEMBER
(Jon Gordon)

1. Set the Example
2. Use Your Strengths to Help the Team
3. Share Positive Contagious Energy
4. Know and Live the Magic Ratio
5. Put the Team First
6. Build Relationships
7. Trust and Be Trusted
8. Hold Them Accountable
9. Be Humble

LEADER VS. BEING IN CHARGE

LEADER	IN CHARGE
We, Us, Ours	I, Me, Mine
Learner	Knows It All
Improves	Maintains
Develops	Evaluates
Win-Win Focus	Must Be Right
Process	Results
Gives Credit	Takes Credit
Inspires	Organizes
Says "Let's Go"	Says "Go"
People	Procedures
Shows How	Knows How
Listener	Quick to Talk
Earns Respect	Expects Respect
Coaches	Criticizes
Enthusiasm	Evokes Fear
Empowers	Controls
Responsibility	Places Blame

12.

AFTERWORD

"I am not what I want to be, I am not what I ought to be, I am not what I am going to be, but thank God, I am not what I used to be."

— Lou Holtz

"The culture precedes positive results. Champions behave like champions before they're champions; they have a winning standard of performance before they are winners."

— Bill Walsh

Culture is a buzz word today. Your coach might set the vision for the program and guide you in a direction toward fulfilling that vision but it is the players that make that vision happen. Players are the people that shape the culture. If you want a championship culture, then it is up to you. A team's culture is like an iceberg in that most people only see the tip of an iceberg. They see your team on game day. They see players in interviews. They see them signing autographs. However, the real culture of a team is what goes on in the locker room, in a hotel room on the road, on the bus or back in the dorms. No matter what your role on the team, you can do something positive to affect the culture of your team.

There will be metaphorical fires in the locker room, bus or dorms to put out. You and your teammates will constantly be faced with the choice of whether you will have a fire extinguisher or lighter fluid. Every player on the team either feeds the fire or extinguishes it. There is no such thing as staying neutral. AS the examples in this book showed, you might not be able to do everything but you can do something. Being a leader is not accidental. Leadership is intentional because it is just influence. Your influence on yourself and others. Each player on the team has to be their own captain. You must be committed to improving yourself so that you can improve the team.

THERE'S A HOLE IN MY SIDEWALK

Through the stories and illustrations in this book, you have learned that everyone can be a leader because leadership is just influence. We also learned that your choices dictate what kind of influence you'll have. Finally, we learned that you must take full responsibility for your choices.

As you have found in your lives or watching others, sometimes we are our own worst enemy. We don't maximize our potential because we are sabotaging ourselves through our negative influence, less than ideal choices or lack of true responsibility. I am reminded of a story by Portia Nelson entitled *There's a Hole in My Sidewalk*,

I walk down the street.
There is a deep hole in the sidewalk.
I fall in.
I am lost... I am helpless.
It isn't my fault.
It takes forever to find a way out.

I walk down the same street.
There is a deep hole in the sidewalk.
I pretend I don't see it.
I fall in again.
I can't believe I am in the same place.
But, it isn't my fault.
It still takes me a long time to get out.

I walk down the same street.
There is a deep hole in the sidewalk.
I see it is there.
I still fall in. It's a habit.
My eyes are open.
I know where I am.
It is my fault. I get out immediately.

I walk down the same street.
There is a deep hole in the sidewalk.
I walk around it.

I walk down another street.

Our decision to be a true person of influence is a continual process. We make positive decisions each day, which lead to good habits which lead to greatness. Success is a choice. What choice will you make today?

You can't do everything, but you can do something. You can influence yourself and influence those closest to you. If you do what's right and influence your closest friends, then they will begin doing what is right. They can then influence other players that they are close to. This ripple effect can have far-reaching effects as you multiply your influence on the team. It is amazing how much can be accomplished on a team when people step up and do the right things.

Little things can add up to big things. Tiny snowflakes can come together to form a snowball or even an avalanche, your small actions can cause an avalanche of change and positive results. Your influence and daily decisions can be like the butterfly effect. Scientists say that the flapping wings of a butterfly can potentially affect the weather in another part of the world because of the change reaction that it sets off. You can be the change agent. You can be the start of a positive change reaction. Lead yourself. Influence others. Change your team.

Throughout this book, you have read many stories that should help you understand how to be a better teammate and leader on your team. Your goal shouldn't be to win the Most Valuable Player award but to be thought of as the best teammate or your team's most valuable leader. Leadership begins with you. You can set the tone for your entire team. If you are a star or captain then you already have an understanding that you must step up and be a leader. If you have a secondary role, you now know that your role is still important and that you can be your team's most valuable leader.

Your point of view of leadership needs to change if you and your team are to achieve its potential. It reminds me of a story from the world of track when for thousands and thousands of years, people thought it was physically impossible to run a sub four-minute mile. It appeared that they were right until May 6, 1954 when a British runner and university student broke that barrier. Roger Bannister's 3:59.4 astounded the running world. It also opened up the flood gates and gave others the confidence and perspective that it could be done. Less than two months later, another runner, Australian John Landy also broke the four-minute barrier. In total 21 runners bested the 4:00 minute mark in the 6 years after Bannister did it. Because the best runners' attitudes changed. They began to adopt the mind-set and beliefs of their peers.

For as long as anyone can remember, the traditional view of leadership is that the coach, the star or the captain is the leader. While they certainly must fulfill their positional leadership responsibilities, they can't lead a team all by themselves. When your point of view toward leadership changes to the understanding that it is merely influence then you realize that anyone can have influence. Teams don't consistently win if they only have one star that is performing. In the same way that stars need teammates to help them succeed on the court, captains, coaches or star players need a total team effort to succeed in the area of leadership.

The stronger your team's leadership is, the better chance you have to be successful. Every team has stars and starters but what differentiates most teams is the intangibles. Those that are associated with leadership. Every team needs players leading themselves, holding each other accountable and encouraging one another so that they can be a true team committed to common goals.

13.

NOTES

CHAPTER 1 (Introduction)

1. John C. Maxwell and Jim Dornan, *Becoming a Person of Influence* (Nashville: Thomas Nelson, Inc., Publishers, 1997), 114-115.

CHAPTER 2 (Foundational Principles)

1. Kevin Templeton, *To The Hilt* (Minneapolis: Two Harbors Press, 2015)
2. Bill Walsh, *The Score Takes Care of Itself* (New York: Penguin Group, 2009)
3. Dale Carnegie, *How to Make Friends and Influence People* (New York: Simon & Schuster, 1936), 102
4. John C. Maxwell, *Developing the Leader Within* (Nashville: Thomas Nelson, Inc., Publishers, 1993), pgs.
5. Pat Williams, *How to Be Like Mike: Life Lessons about Basketball's Best* (Deerfield Beach, FL: Health Communications, Incorporated, 2001), pgs.
6. Keith Sharon, "The Western Oregon home run that won an ESPY and changed college softball forever", *The Oregonian*, December 16, 2014, http://www.oregonlive.com/sports/index.ssf/2014/12/the_western_oregon_home_run_th.html

CHAPTER 3 (Leadership Defined)

1. Tony Gallegos, "True Story: Little Things Make A Big Difference", *The Mortgage Cicerone* blog, July 23, 2007, https://tonygallegos.wordpress.com/2007/07/23/true-story-little-things-make-a-big-difference/
2. Patrick Hayes, "O.J. Mayo says Chauncey Billups is the best leader in the NBA", *MLive.com*, October 21, 2009, http://blog.mlive.com/fullcourtpress/2009/10/oj_mayo_says_chauncey_billups.html
3. Jonathan Abrams, "The Professional", *Grantland.com*, December 12, 2012, http://grantland.com/features/it-always-easy-chauncey-billups-stopped-putting-together-one-nba-best-careers/

4. John Walters, *The Same River Twice: A Season with Geno Auriemma and the Connecticut Huskies* (New York: Junkerhalter Publishing, 2002)

5. Mechelle Voepel, "Five reasons UConn has been so good for so long", *ESPN.com*, January 12, 2017, http://www.espn.com/womens-college-basketball/story/_/id/18458063/how-connecticut-huskies-sustained-their-success

6. Julie Greco, "10 years later, George Boiardi's legacy carries on", *Ezra Update*, March 2014, http://ezramagazine.cornell.edu/Update/March14/EU.Boiardi.10.years.html

7. Bill Chastain, "Zobrist's leadership comes 'chrome'-free", *MLB.com*, September 20, 2013, http://m.rays.mlb.com/news/article/61137904/

8. Lou Holtz, *Winning Every Day: The Game Plan for Success* (New York: HarperCollins Publishers, 1999)

9. Jon Gordon and Mike Smith, *You Win in the Locker Room First* (Hoboken, NJ: John Wiley & Sons, Inc., 2015)

CHAPTER 4 (Leading Yourself)

1. Paul Newberry, "For Falcons star Jones, the only stat that matters is wins", *TheScore.com*, November 19, 2015, https://www.thescore.com/news/886986

2. Zach Buckley, "Former Teammates, Rivals Still Vividly Recall Ray Allen's Defining Moment", *Bleacher Report*, November 2, 2016, http://bleacherreport.com/articles/2673450-former-teammates-opponents-still-vividly-recall-ray-allens-defining-moment

3. Dan Devine, "Stephen Curry ejected, hits fan with mouthpiece in Game 6 meltdown", *Yahoo.com*, June 16, 2016, https://sports.yahoo.com/blogs/nba-ball-dont-lie/stephen-curry-ejected--hits-fan-with-mouthpiece-in-game-6-meltdown-035225854.html

4. "Steelers Ben Roethlisberger 'Is 'A Little Disappointed' With Antonio Brown", January 17, 2017, *93.7 the Fan* interview, http://pittsburgh.cbslocal.com/2017/01/17/ben-roethlisberger-is-a-little-disappointed-with-antonio-brown/)

5. Jason King, "From Walk-on to UNC's NCAA Tournament Hero: Luke Maye's Amazing Story", *Bleacher Report*, March 27, 2017, (http://bleacherreport.com/articles/2700182-from-walk-on-to-uncs-ncaa-tournament-hero-luke-mayes-amazing-story)

6. Lou Holtz, *Winning Every Day: The Game Plan for Success* (New York: HarperCollins Publishers, 1999),

7. Darren Poke, "The Retiring Carpenter – A Story About the Life We Build for Ourselves", *Better Life Coaching Blog*, September 23, 2011, https://betterlifecoachingblog.com/2011/09/23/the-retiring-carpenter-a-story-about-the-life-we-build-for-ourselves-2/

CHAPTER 5 (Leading Others)

1. Kathy Caudill, "What is hazing?", National Federation of State High School Associations website, July 24, 2014, https://www.nfhs.org/sports-resource-content/starwhat-is-hazing
2. Kevin Templeton, *To The Hilt* (Minneapolis: Two Harbors Press, 2015), 130
3. Josh Weinfuss, "Cardinals teammates influenced by Larry Fitzgerald on, off the field", *ESPN.com*, December 28, 2016, http://www.espn.com/blog/arizona-cardinals/post/_/id/24149/cardinals-teammates-influenced-by-larry-fitzgerald-on-off-the-field
4. Bill Walsh, *The Score Takes Care of Itself* (New York: Penguin Group, 2009), pgs.
5. Bob Starkey, "The Jerry Rice Work Ethic", *HoopThoughts Blog*, November 6, 2008, http://hoopthoughts.blogspot.com/2008/11/jerry-rice-work-ethic.html
6. Vaughn McClure, "Falcons' Julio Jones strives to have Jerry Rice-like work ethic", *ESPN.com*, January 5, 2017, http://www.espn.com/blog/nfcsouth/post/_/id/66861/falcons-julio-jones-all-about-having-jerry-rice-like-work-ethic
7. Paul Newberry, "For Falcons star Jones, the only stat that matters is wins", *TheScore.com*, November 19, 2015, https://www.thescore.com/news/886986

CHAPTER 6 (Leading Regardless of Role)

1. John C. Maxwell, *The 5 Levels of leadership* (New York: Center Street, Hachette Book Group, 2011)
2. John C. Maxwell, *The 21 Irrefutable Laws of Leadership: 10th Anniversary Edition* (Nashville: Thomas Nelson, Inc., Publishers, 2007)
3. Biography.com Editors, "Harriet Tubman", *Biography.com*, April 27, 2017, https://www.biography.com/people/harriet-tubman-9511430
4. Chantel Jennings, "Monmouth bench becomes a star attraction", *ESPN.com*, December 1, 2015, http://www.espn.com/blog/collegebasketballnation/post/_/id/109330/monmouth-bench-becomes-a-star-attraction
5. Adam Kilgore, "Monmouth's benchwarmers are the most entertaining attraction in college basketball", *Washington Post*, December 14, 2015, https://www.washingtonpost.com/news/sports/wp/2015/12/14/at-monmouth-basketball-games-the-bench-warmers-are-the-cool-kids/?utm_term=.1cc2d2e97f6b
6. Elaine Quijano, "Monmouth University's basketball stars are the bench warmers", *CBSnews.com*, March 17, 2016, http://www.cbsnews.com/news/ncaa-monmouth-bench-university-basketball-stars-are-sitting-on-the-sidelines-march-madness/

7. Jim Tressel, *The Winners Manual* (Carol Stream, IL: Tyndale House Publishers, Inc., 2008)

8. Doug Farrar, "Emmitt Smith steals the show with emotional enshrinement speech", *Yahoo Sports*, August 8, 2010, https://sports.yahoo.com/nfl/blog/shutdown_corner/post/Emmitt-Smith-steals-the-show-with-emotional-ensh?urn=nfl,260951

9. Doug Haller, "20 years later: An Arizona Wildcats championship to remember", *AZCentral.com*, March 13, 2017, http://www.azcentral.com/story/sports/ncaab/final-four/2017/03/13/20-years-later-arizona-wildcats-championship-remember/98953054/

10. John O'Keefe, "Whiz-kid Coach At age 25, hoops-obsessed Arizona assistant Josh Pastner is on the fast track to a top job", *Sports Illustrated*, February 3, 2003, https://www.si.com/vault/2003/02/03/336932/whiz-kid-coach-at-age-25-hoops-obsessed-arizona-assistant-josh-pastner-is-on-the-fast-track-to-a-top-job

11. Nathan Baird, "Former Purdue basketball walk-ons now vocal leaders", *Journal & Courier*, August 27, 2014, http://www.jconline.com/story/sports/college/purdue/basketball/2014/08/23/purdue-mens-basketball-walk-leadership/14513167/

12. Nathan Baird, "Purdue senior Neal Beshears rewarded with wins", *Journal & Courier*, March 6, 2015, http://www.indystar.com/story/sports/college/purdue/2015/03/06/purdue-neal-beshears-senior-night/24491133/

CHAPTER 7 (Positional Leadership)

1. Bill Walsh, *The Score Will Take Care of Itself* (New York: Penguin Group, 2009), 197

2. Joe Giglio, "Derek Jeter's Former Teammates Discuss His Leadership, Legacy and More", April 1, 2014, *Bleacher Report*, http://bleacherreport.com/articles/2012761-derek-jeters-former-teammates-discuss-his-leadership-legacy-and-more

3. Adam Bryant, "Walt Bettinger of Charles Schwab: You've Got to Open Up to Move Up", *New York Times*, February 4, 2016, https://www.nytimes.com/2016/02/07/business/walt-bettinger-of-charles-schwab-youve-got-to-open-up-to-move-up.html

4. Alan Williams, *Walk-On: Life from the end of the bench* (New Heights Press, 2006)

5. Brian Cronin, "Did Reese really embrace Robinson in 47", *ESPN.com*, August 15, 2013, http://www.espn.com/blog/playbook/fandom/post/_/id/20917/did-reese-really-embrace-robinson-in-47

6. Dick Devenzio, *Runnin' The Show*, (Australia: Bridgeway Books, 2006), 119-126

CHAPTER 8 (Verbal Leadership)

1. Phil Ervin, "Follow the leader: Lynx's Moore becoming more vocal", *FoxSports.com*, May 1, 2014, http://www.foxsports.com/north/story/follow-the-leader-lynx-s-moore-becoming-more-vocal-050114

2. Tobias Fredberg, "Why Good Leaders Pass the Cred and Take the Blame", *The Harvard Business Review*, October 6, 2011, https://hbr.org/2011/10/why-good-leaders-pass-the-cred

CHAPTER 9 (Teamwork)

1. Tom Kendra, "Bo Schembechler's legendary The Team speech still rings true today in high school football", *The Muskegon Chronicle*, August 24, 2011, http://www.mlive.com/sports/muskegon/index.ssf/2011/08/bo_schembechlers_legendary_the.html

2. Shane Dreiling, "Old Warwick", *Life Lessons in Words* Blog, July 7, 2010, http://wordsfortheyoung.blogspot.com/2010/07/old-warwick.html

3. Jon Gordon, *The Energy Bus: 10 Rules to Fuel Your Life, Work, and Team with Positive Energy* (Hoboken, NJ: John Wiley & Sons, Inc., 2007), 73

4. Keith Langlois, "The Goin' to Work Pistons: 5 fingers became an iron fist", *NBA.com*, June 16, 2014, http://www.nba.com/pistons/features/goin-work-pistons-5-fingers-became-iron-fist/

5. Doug Sibor, "The 50 Most Unsportsmanlike Acts in Sports History", *Complex.com*, July 5, 2013, http://www.complex.com/sports/2013/07/most-unsportsmanlike-acts-in-sports-history/

6. Barry Temkin, "'Fab' Also Applies To This Role Player", *Chicago Tribune*, April 2, 1993

7. Andrew Joseph, "Twitter reacts to Tony Romo's emotional support for Dak Prescott as Cowboys starting QB", *USAtoday.com*, November 15, 2016, http://ftw.usatoday.com/2016/11/twitter-reacts-tony-romo-emotional-support-dak-prescott-cowboys-starting-qb

8. Channing Frye, "Let's Enjoy This Wonderful French Toast", *The Players Tribune*, August 8, 2106, https://www.theplayerstribune.com/channing-frye-cavaliers-nba-champions-heart/

9. Michael Singer, "Tristan Thompson played starring role in Cavs' Game 6 win", *USA Today*, June 17, 2016, https://www.usatoday.com/story/sports/nba/playoffs/2016/06/17/tristan-thompson-lebron-james-cavaliers-warriors-finals/86025524/

10. Kevin Templeton, *To The Hilt* (Minneapolis: Two Harbors Press, 2015)

CHAPTER 10 (Outwork Your Talent)

1. Joe McDonald, "Red Sox recall better times", *ESPN.com*, September 26, 2012, http://www.espn.com/boston/mlb/story/_/id/8426600/boston-red-sox-recall-winning-chemistry-2004

2. Stu Hackel, "NHL playoffs: Playing in pain is a timeless tradition", *SI.com*, June 4, 2013, https://www.si.com/nhl/2013/06/04/nhl-playoffs-playing-pain-stories

3. Benjamin Hochman, "Broncos QB Peyton Manning works "as if he never had a penny", *Denver Post*, August 12, 2014, http://www.denverpost.com/2014/08/12/hochman-broncos-qb-peyton-manning-works-as-if-he-never-had-a-penny/

4. David Maraniss, *When Pride Still Mattered: A Life Of Vince Lombardi* (New York: Simon & Schuster, 2000)

5. Vince Lombardi, "What It Takes to be Number One", *VinceLombardi.com*, http://www.vincelombardi.com/number-one.html

6. Neil Paine, "Where This Year's Cavs Rank Among LeBron's NBA Finals Supporting Casts", *FiveThirtyEight*, June 1, 2015, https://fivethirtyeight.com/datalab/where-this-years-cavs-rank-among-lebrons-nba-finals-supporting-casts/

7. Mark Shaw, *Larry Legend* (Create Space, 2011)

8. Mark Lamport-Stokes, "Bryant built Hall of Fame career with tireless work ethic", Reuters, April 14, 2016, http://www.reuters.com/article/us-nba-lakers-bryant-newsmaker-idUSKCN0XB0DV

9. Larry Bird, *Drive: The Story of my Life* (New York: Bantam Books, 1990), 283-284

CHAPTER 11 (Quick Hitters)

1. John C. Maxwell, *The 17 Indisputable Laws of Teamwork* (Nashville: Thomas Nelson, Inc., Publishers, 2001)

2. Jon Gordon, "9 Ways to Be a Great Team Member", http://www.jongordon.com/positive-tip-team-member.html

3. Bruce Brown, Captains - 7 Ways to Lead Your Team: Be First...Be Last (Proactive Coaching, 2014), pgs. 4-18

4. John C. Maxwell, *The 15 Invaluable Laws of Growth* (Nashville: Thomas Nelson, Inc., Publishers, 2012)

5. Colin Powell, *My American Journey* (New York: Random House, 1995), 613

6. Stephen Covery, *7 Habits of Highly Effective People* (New York: Free Press Publishing, 1989),

7. Craig Hillier, "Avoid the Top 10 Mistakes Team Captains Make", http://craighillier.com/craigs-leadership-articles/

CHAPTER 12 (Afterword)

1. Portia Nelson, *There's a Hole in My Sidewalk: The Romance of Self-Discovery* (New York: Simon & Schuster, 1989), pgs.
2. Matt Frazier, "What We Mortals Can Learn From the 4-Minute Mile", *NoMeatAthlete.com*, http://www.nomeatathlete.com/4-minute-mile-certainty

MAXIMIZE YOUR POTENTIAL

Success is a choice ... What choice will you make today?

If you are interested in having Jamy Bechler speak to your team or conduct a training session to increase leadership skills or help create a championship culture, please contact speaking@jamybechler.com.

Connect with Jamy at:
Facebook: JamyBechlerLeadership
Twitter: @CoachBechler
Instagram: @CoachBechler
Linkedin: JamyBechler
Website: JamyBechler.com

To order bulk copies of The Leadership Playbook for your large group or team, please contact support@TheLeadershipPlaybook.com.

Get free access to additional resources by going to www.TheLeadershipPlaybook.com and using code "online". There are discussions questions, handouts, and other valuable tools to help you take your leadership and success to a higher level.

Made in the USA
Columbia, SC
27 July 2017